Mother Angelica

MOTHER ANGELICA

✳

Her Life Story

DAN O'NEILL

CROSSROAD · NEW YORK

1986

The Crossroad Publishing Company
370 Lexington Avenue, New York, N.Y. 10017

Library of Congress Cataloging in Publication Data

O'Neill, Dan.
Mother Angelica : her life story.

1. M. Angelica, Mother. 2. Poor Clares—United
States—Biography. 3. Eternal Word Television
Network. 4. Television in religion—United States.
I. Title.
BX4705.M124054   1986   271'.973'024 [B]   86-4213
ISBN 0-8245-0742-8

To the memory of
Sister David of the Infant Jesus
April 23, 1899—August 22, 1982

Contents

Acknowledgments

There are many who have made the present work possible through their supportive roles. Sister M. Raphael, assistant to Mother Angelica at Our Lady of the Angels Monastery, provided invaluable assistance in the preparation of archive material, photographs and interviews. Also, special thanks to the Sisters who assisted in various ways through interviews, written commentary and, of course, prayer.

Below are others who have contributed significantly to this work.

Ginny Dominick
Dr. Maury Sheridan
Ellsworth Culver
Pam Borgen
Lawana Norman
Mary Lu McKnight

Preface

It seems I cannot escape the touch of St. Francis of Assisi. I first felt his "presence" while driving a Landrover through the beautiful Umbrian countryside in the very heart of Italy in the spring of 1973. Farmland and vineyards fill the valley below the town of Assisi. The lush, green landscape is breathtaking, surrounding the legendary mountainside hometown of the little saint who changed the world. Historians claim it looks much the same now as it did the day Francis was born in 1182.

Over the next few years I lived and traveled extensively in the Middle East. Christians visiting the Holy Land find religious holy sites a very special part of their pilgrimage. Jerusalem is, of course, a particular high point and is full of holy places. These locations have been assigned to the stewardship of the Franciscans, many of whom may readily be seen scurrying about the "Golden City" in their distinctive brown habits and sandals. This was yet another encounter with Francis, whose life journey created its own fair share of hallowed places, monuments and religious relics.

In 1978 I discovered the peace prayer of St. Francis:

Lord, make me an instrument of your peace.
Where there is hatred, let me sow love.

1

Where there is injury, pardon.
Where there is doubt, faith.
Where there is despair, hope.
Where there is darkness, light.
Where there is sadness, joy.
O Divine Master, grant that I may not so much seek
To be consoled, as to console,
To be understood, as to understand,
To be loved, as to love.
For it is in giving that we receive,
It is in pardoning that we are pardoned,
It is in dying that we are born to eternal life.

St. Francis of Assisi established his religious order in April of 1209 under Pope Innocent III. He called it the Order of Friars Minor, which translated means, "little brothers." Francis was radically committed to living the gospel of Christ, embracing "Lady Poverty" and building God's church. Two other Franciscan orders were subsequently developed, one by Clare of Assisi who became the first woman to follow the example of Francis. Poor Clares, the Second Order of St. Francis, seek to live a life of cloistered, contemplative prayer.

Of particular interest to me—an interest I share with millions—is one Franciscan nun, Mother Angelica. Even now, as I write this story, Francis seems to be peering over my shoulder cheering me on. This is a story he wants told—a story of radical Christian faith in action.

The Franciscan Nuns of the Most Blessed Sacrament, to which Mother Angelica belongs, is a pontifical order of Poor Clares founded upon a ministry of perpetual adoration of the Blessed Sacrament. It was formed in Paris, France, in 1854 by Capuchin friar John Baptist Heurlant and Mother Mary St. Clare Bouillevaux. Members engaged in various forms of ministry within their cloistered communities.

From this unlikely setting—the quiet cloister of the monastery—Mother Angelica launched her own nationwide television network, EWTN (Eternal Word Television Network). She has succeeded despite overwhelming odds and predictions of failure by the "experts." From the Blessed Sacrament to a blessed satellite, from the sanctuary to the studio, the Sisters of Our Lady of the Angels Monastery in Irondale, Alabama, share the good news across the nation with "Mother" leading them.

But just exactly how does this high-powered, electronic-media ministry fit into the traditional quietude of a contemplative Franciscan order of nuns?

Perhaps more than we might at first realize. Francis's entire life was dedicated to *communication*—sharing and living the gospel in such a powerful way that the foundations of the medieval church were shaken with spiritual renewal. The little troubadour continues to challenge our world and touch our lives for Christ through his followers, among whom is Mother Mary Angelica, the little nun who could.

In April of 1985, I sat with Mother Angelica in the dining room of her monastery discussing the manuscript that would become this book. Of course I probed into her past with the standard writer's questions about childhood and family.

"Just how much time are we going to spend looking back into the past?" she demanded. "You know, I'm really much more interested in what's going on today—or better yet, tomorrow! Let's get on with it!"

Let's face it, I thought to myself, this woman isn't interested in a classic biography. She has no time to rest on her accomplishments or wistfully recall the good old days. She is totally committed to the critical path that lies ahead: sharing God's love through the medium of television. There is little time for looking back. Still, a picture of her life is important in understanding what forces have come together to create this extraordinary person. The picture is important to me, you, and the other millions who are touched by her.

I can see Francis smiling.

Dan O'Neill

Foreword

When I first met Mother Angelica after entering our monastery in Canton, Ohio, she was just another Sister among many. Then one day she sat down to talk to me about some problems I was having, and suddenly I realized I was sitting opposite a spiritual giant. Her guidance opened doors of the spiritual life into states of prayer I never knew existed. She began to uncover all the fears, anxieties, confusions and heartaches that I could not articulate. Never have I gone to her with a problem that she was not able to unravel. She would urge me on to greater sacrifices, patience and effort.

I watched her own struggle with pain, her desire to build a monastery in the South and her many disappointments. When she was sick in the infirmary after her back operation, and all her dreams for the future seemed dashed to the ground, she was there cheering up her visitors. I knew as I listened to her that she had such an intense love for God that one day the world would know what He had done in her soul.

Mother is a great storyteller. What makes her stories so funny is that they actually happened the way she tells them. One evening she came into the refectory laughing during dinner and told us about the young man on the phone who began giving all his reasons for talking directly to Mother Angelica.

When she said, "This is Mother," he became so flustered and stuttered so badly he couldn't talk.

Another time she was in a shopping center when a woman approached her and said, "Are you Sisters from the monastery?" Mother nodded yes and the lady continued, "Please tell Mother Angelica I said hello—I'm one of her best friends!"

Here at Our Lady of the Angels Monastery near Birmingham, Alabama, there is always a sense of excitement. We constantly find ourselves clustering around Mother to hear what our newest project might be. Her enthusiasm is contagious, and she has a brilliant mind and good common sense. Where others would find an excuse to give up, Mother will always find a way if she believes something is for the glory of God or for the common good of the community.

Mother Angelica's ingenuity and drive have always sparked our community into action. Whether it's a do-it-yourself cabinet or a macaroni maker, Mother is there with the saw, nails, varnish and paint (she antiqued all the woodwork in the chapel herself from the cruet table to the altar). I've watched her lay floor tile, fix doorknobs, build chicken coops, supervise a shrine for the Pietà, build a twenty-foot stone wall, lay sod, sand and seal.

One Sunday she came to help me in the kitchen. When we were done the kitchen was a shambles (the disorder bordered on the ridiculous) but we sure had delicious cherry tarts! In the thick of the laughter and flurry you'll always find Mother Angelica.

Mother never indiscriminately assigns the day's work. It is always carefully fitted to each Sister's capacity and ability. With great care and concern she analyzes each one's ability and subsequently expects full cooperation.

Every book Mother has written was scrawled on a yellow tablet, usually before the Blessed Sacrament where she receives her inspiration. Then it is brought to our daily lesson and read one page at a time until finished. Sometimes we spend days on a page until her meaning is absolutely clear to each Sister. She then pursues publication and distribution for her booklets so others may benefit from them.

Her tenacity and perseverance are remarkable. Nothing stands in her way once she sees that God is leading her. I remember when the stapler/trimmer arrived for our printing operation. Mother wanted it put in the hallway so she could start working on it while the new press room was being finished. It was an exasperating machine, but using wrenches, screwdrivers and hand cranks, she totally mastered the equipment after staying up several nights in a row.

One day Mother had just returned from having an operation on her foot when a Sister came to tell her the stapler/trimmer was chewing up the books. She limped to the print shop on a very sore foot, began cranking, testing and adjusting to make it right. I attempted to persuade her to leave it to the service man. As I walked in the door I saw a look on her face of anguished pain like I had never seen before. The crank had slipped from her hand, dropping directly on that fresh incision. I could feel all the nerves in my body tingle empathetically as the Sisters told me what had just happened. Still, she did not abandon the effort until the machine was back in perfect working condition.

We began the Eternal Word Television ministry in a garage because, as Mother explains to everyone, "I lost my temper." She called a long-time friend who worked with iron and asked him to come out and look at the studio she was building. When he arrived she showed him the walls going up and told him she needed some trussed beams to hold up the roof. After they had talked a while she took him around to see the press room. As he was about to leave he asked another question about the new studio and then remarked casually, "By the way, where are the plans?"

"Oh," she said, "here!" Grabbing a sheet of offset printing paper in the press room, she drew a square to represent the studio and then made two lines across it to indicate where she wanted the trussed beams. "There!" she said proudly with feigned innocence. His mouth dropped open and his eyes widened.

"These are the plans?" he asked.

"Those are the plans and that's what I want," she replied. In a daze he made his way to the telephone and I overheard him tell his foreman as he stood there with the paper dangling from his limp arm, "You won't believe the 'plans' I have in my hands!"

When he finished his conversation, Mother started laughing and told him he could frame that drawing and hang it in his shop. "Tell people that you are so good you work from plans like these!"

We Sisters often marvel at her childlike trust and hope in God when everything seems to be going against her. With the high pressure of TV broadcast expenses every month, and not knowing where the money will come from, she keeps pushing forward. I have watched Mother keep self-control in front of the Sisters when her heart was tortured with the fear of losing the network because she didn't have the funds for the monthly payment. Though she shares everything with us, she tries not to burden us with her own weight of responsibility.

One evening about half an hour before she was due downstairs for the "Live" show, she finally broke down and cried. We all cried with her. She could see no way out of her dilemma, but she was determined that she would never ask for funds on the air. She did not want to use the time for anything but teaching people about Jesus.

"God will provide," she told us. "I want to prove to people that His providence takes care of us." With that she went down to the studio and never said a word on or off the air about her financial predicament. After the show she confided to me that she had no way to get the money we needed. She had exhausted all known possibilities.

"Mother, you've got to go on the air and tell the people what is happening. They have a right to know that the network is in jeopardy, that we can lose everything," I said. "They have an obligation to help us. The network is for them, not us. It's not fair to let it all go down the drain without telling the family. They're part of God's providence too."

Finally she agreed that the next night she would go on live between programs and share with her listeners the tremendous burden she was carrying. After several weeks word got around and people began to send contributions; many thanked her for sharing her problems with them. They had no idea the needs were so desperate. Now, with the help of our growing television family, Mother is still proving to be a powerful witness to God's providence.

Mother Angelica's life story will appeal to people because it is so filled with the joys, sorrows, upheavals and weaknesses that we all face in our lives. Her experiences are encouraging to common people everywhere.

It is the hope of the Sisters that this book will give courage and strength to those who feel incapable of changing things both in the world and in their lives

Sister M. Raphael
Our Lady of the Angels Monastery
Irondale, Alabama

CHAPTER ONE

---*---

The Way of Sorrows

Fourteen-year-old Rita Rizzo fought back tears as she wrestled the old Packard through the crowded streets of Canton, Ohio. The mid-summer sun of July 1938 was already beginning to set, the temperature continued to hover in the high, humid eighties and still her errands were far from finished. Who could blame her for thinking her life was like a bad dream?

Maturity had been forced on Rita. She had been driving since she was only eleven, delivering suits to patrons of her mother's faltering dry-cleaning business. These were gritty post-depression days, and the mood was somber in the Italian immigrant section of town. People on the streets were tense; the talk was of war in far away countries. Everyone was anxious about the rumors. Everyone, that is, except Rita.

She was fighting her own war—a war of simple, basic survival. She and her mother, Mae, were trying to make a living against the odds, but they seemed to be losing ground daily. Usually Mae tried to accompany Rita on delivery routes, but today she was too tired to leave home. Depressed and distraught, Mae was beginning to lean on Rita more and more. Increased responsibility weighed heavily upon Rita as it would on any child her age. And this particular day seemed a truly bad one. Not one customer was able to pay his cleaning bill

10

for the second day in a row. How will I face Mother tonight, she asked herself through the swelling lump in her throat. How can we go on like this?

After her last delivery, Rita decided on a circuitous route back home. She needed more time to think. The situation was tough. But so was she and besides, she reasoned, things will look up tomorrow. The tentative seeds of youthful faith were already planted deeply within her soul. In spite of the harsh realities, Rita believed she would somehow find a way. This faith would become a way of life for her.

Barely able to peer over the steering wheel, Rita Rizzo took the long way home and reflected on her troubled life.

Her mother, Mae Helen Gianfrancisco, was born on April 23, 1899, to an Italian immigrant family in Canton. She was one of eleven children. From early childhood Mae's life was filled with adversity and bitter disappointments. She possessed musical talent, striking good looks, and a fiery, independent spirit. Some of the older generation openly called her a hopeless rebel.

The significant strike against her came when her parents forced her to quit school in the sixth grade. She felt rejected, betrayed and wounded, hurts she would not forget for the rest of her life. Could there be any hope for her future? Education meant everything to Mae. Being pulled out of school was a tragic, negative turning point in her life.

These conflicts marked Mae, leaving interior scars that would later shape her life. She also mourned the loss of four young siblings to illness, then later survived the devastating Spanish flu epidemic in 1918 that claimed thousands of lives, many of them in her neighborhood. These events put her into a chronically depressed and pessimistic state.

But her unhappiness seemed to end when she married John

Rizzo on September 8, 1921. Their joyous marriage celebration was full of Italian ethnic tradition and Catholic ritual. An Italian whose family came from Calabria in the western arch of the Italian boot, Rizzo was strong and handsome. This was surely a new start for Mae.

Unfortunately, her happiness was to be short-lived. Within two years, their marriage had turned ugly. When Mae learned she was pregnant, she rushed to tell John the joyful news. Anticipating a happy and joyous response, she was greeted instead with coldness and indifference. Her husband's reaction came as a cruel shock. She had never witnessed this side of his personality before.

Their life was further complicated by John's mother, who moved into the Rizzo home at Mae's invitation. Mae attempted to accommodate her by extending hospitality in spite of her difficulties. This act of kindness only created more complications. Mae became the victim of her mother-in-law's harsh, relentless criticism.

John and Mae's only child, Rita Antoinette Rizzo, was born on April 20, 1923. One day she would be known to millions as Mother Mary Angelica or simply "Mother" to her friends and coworkers. She was a healthy and, at least temporarily, happy baby, her mother's joy. Rita was born into a household now full of turbulence and emotional instability. The difficult marriage, combined with Mae's personal history of emotional problems, stacked the deck against the infant.

Even before Rita's arrival, the Rizzos' domestic situation had begun to deteriorate. During a family flare-up, complicated by the presence of Mae's domineering mother-in-law who turned her son against his wife, John suddenly moved out, leaving Mae and Rita alone. He disappeared completely from their lives for more than two years. His desertion left mother and daughter with only each other to share grief, rejection and terrifying uncertainty. Where would they live? How would they survive?

Rita was thinking about her childhood as she drove the long way home. Suddenly she was jarred back to the reality of the bustling, early evening traffic by a sharp pain in her stomach. She would not mention the pain to anyone. There were more than enough other problems to go around.

She was nearing the apartment now. As she came closer to home she cheered herself on, reminding herself that in spite of everything, she was working with her mother and they were at least able to feed themselves, even if only one day at a time. And there would be a month or two more of warm weather, which was better than the freezing nights she spent each winter in a cramped apartment without heat. Thank God for small blessings, she thought to herself. Again, her mind drifted back to earlier years, years compressed into fleeting yet poignant memories.

Her parents' divorce was finalized when Rita was six years old. One day, shortly thereafter, her maternal grandfather approached her with a troubled look on his face. It was obvious that something was wrong. "You'd better pray, Rita," he scowled. "We are going to the courthouse to see the judge today. Pray that he will give you to your mother and not to your father." She was frightened beyond words, beyond even tears.

Immediately Rita hid in an obscure niche behind the icebox and stayed there until her mother and grandfather returned from their court appointment.

"Rita!" her grandfather called. "Rita, where are you?" he repeated. "The judge said we could keep you!" She came out from her hiding place into her mother's arms sobbing. Wasn't this already more than a child should have to bear? And it was to be only the beginning.

✳

Today Mother Angelica looks back on those days and shakes her head remembering.

"After the divorce, things went from bad to worse. We tried living with my mother's parents—you can just imagine—a house full of children and here we come straight off the streets. There wasn't much room so we slept in the attic, which was definitely not meant for human habitation. I mean, there was no room. And cold! It was terribly cold that winter. I remember one night during a storm the wind blew the windows open with a resounding crash and snow literally blew in on top of us! Needless to say, that living situation was not to last long."

When life seemed especially desperate, Mae turned to her parish priest, Father Riccardi, pastor of St. Anthony's Catholic Church, for consolation and advice. She and Rita were uplifted through the kindness of this man, who became a true and trusted friend to them. He was open, supportive and available—like the angel of the Lord to Rita and her mother—a channel of blessing God had mercifully opened to them in their sufferings. As an act of gratitude to Father Riccardi, and out of her deepening love of God, Mae volunteered her time to numerous church activities including parish dinners and special events to benefit St. Anthony's Church. Because Mae had so little money, this seemed the only means of offering something meaningful to the Lord—her time and work.

"What would I do without you and Rita?" Father Riccardi once asked, a broad smile gracing his ruggedly handsome face.

"No, Father. The real question is, what would *we* do without you?" Mae retorted instantly.

"Oh come now, Mae! You and Rita would be taken care of quite nicely, I'm certain. Remember, you are in the hands of the Lord. Don't ever forget that!" he exclaimed.

St. Anthony's Church was located in the tougher part of town, turf that undisputedly belonged to the Black Hands, a local arm of the Mafia. This organization had claimed a chunk of Canton territory through bootlegging, protection rackets, bribery and other classic gangland maneuvers. No one stood in their way.

According to street gossip, the Black Hands had money invested in the illegal liquor trade, one of their primary sources of illicit income. One evening, at a clandestine Black Hands strategy meeting, the leadership met to discuss the growing problem of storing a shipment of whiskey—hundreds of bottles worth thousands on the black market. They finally decided that the cases of whiskey should be stashed in trenches dug on a remote section of St. Anthony's schoolyard. Laughter filled the smoke-laden room as the plans were made. Who would ever think to look on church property, they howled. It was a perfect idea and would be carried out by hirelings under the cover of darkness.

Somehow word of the plot was leaked to Father Riccardi, who was not about to ignore criminal activities of any kind, including those of the dreaded Black Hands. Through an intermediary, the priest passed the message that continued use of church land to conceal liquor by the mobsters would result in his immediate installment of bright floodlights to disrupt the late-night excavations.

"Mind your own business, Father, and no one gets hurt," came the threatening reply.

"This *is* my business," the undaunted priest responded. Within twenty-four hours he erected a battery of lights that, as planned, illuminated the area in dispute but also sealed his fate with the leaders of the crime syndicate.

Father Riccardi became a bit more careful with his routine at first. He refrained from walking the streets in the evenings and stayed away from blind alleys. But life in the parish continued and Father engaged in his priestly activities with little interruption. He especially enjoyed baptisms because this sacrament represented new life in the parish and in the church at large. On March 10, 1929, he welcomed a young mother and father to the church sanctuary for the baptism of their new baby. The parents and a few friends and relatives gathered around the baptismal font as Father Riccardi poured the blessed water over the newborn's head. Suddenly, through the small knot of ceremony participants, a slightly built, cloaked figure—a woman—emerged with her hands thrust deeply into her heavy coat pockets. Without warning, and before anyone could react, she pulled a revolver and fired away point-blank at the priest who collapsed, mortally wounded, his blood spilling upon the floor in a large pool. Amid the shouts and screams, the silent, anonymous intruder swept through the side exit.

Father Riccardi lost his life in the service of his church family. Rita and Mae were hysterical when they heard the news. This grief seemed too great to bear.

After Father Riccardi's death, Mae plunged into despair from which there seemed no possible return. Rita attempted to bolster her mother's flagging spirits. After all, Rita reasoned, aren't priests to be a model of Christ—His representatives on earth? And hadn't Jesus encountered His murderers as He served His chosen ones during His own ministry? Yes. He had spilled His precious blood at the hands of dark forces but just as surely had overcome the shroud of death through a spectacular resurrection. Rita began to search for the resurrection in their own lives. "I will fear no evil . . ." Rita recited to herself the words of a Psalm she had recently memorized.

Incidents of bad luck, like so many bricks, piled up around them—roadblocking their lives at every turn. They were forced to move repeatedly. "We were like a pair of refugees," Mother says of their vagabond life-style. "We were poor, hungry and barely surviving on odd jobs before Mother learned the dry-cleaning business as an apprentice to a Jewish tailor in our area. Even then, we pinched pennies just to keep food on the table."

But poverty was not their only problem. Mae reached a

state of suicidal depression, overwhelmed by the circumstances of their lives. Rita had no choice: She had to take charge of their survival. She learned to chart her own destiny in a contrary sea. There was little time for self-pity—and even less for the recreation enjoyed by most young people her age.

Because survival came first, school work went undone. Grades plunged. Teachers frowned in obvious disapproval. Her years at St. Anthony Catholic Grade School left few fond memories. Not only did she dislike school in general, but she also didn't get along well at all with the nuns who showed an obvious preference for other children. A confrontation when she was in the sixth grade permanently separated her from the parochial-school system.

It was a cool, crisp Monday. Rita ran into the classroom already happily anticipating the Christmas party scheduled for later in the week. Traditionally, each student received a gift from the teacher and, of course, each one wondered what they would receive. Mondays were especially lean days for Rita and her mother because it was tithe day—the occasion for offering money to the church through the school system. And money was a scarce commodity in the Rizzo household.

Rita handed her teacher the damp and worn one-dollar bill that she had clutched tightly in her hand all the way to school. This Monday offering was her only chance to give a gift to God, even though it was but a "widow's mite." Rita noted her teacher's cool response and then dismissed it. God, she reasoned, would surely take notice and bless her and Mae for their sacrifice.

On the day of the class Christmas celebration, Rita and her schoolmates chattered happily. Between Christmas carols they giggled and wondered what gifts were in store. Finally, the gifts were distributed by roll call. Tommy Anthony received a pencil box. Annette Benedict held her brand new diary up in pride. The gifts were good ones, and Rita could hardly wait for hers. Finally, her big moment came as her name was called.

She held out her hand politely with all the restraint she could muster.

"Thank you, Sister," she whispered as she placed the circular, brightly wrapped package on her desk. She opened the gift to find a well-used Yo-Yo, its string knotted and soiled. Her cheeks flushed red in anger and confusion. Now Rita remembered the look on her teacher's face the Monday before the party when she had turned over her old dollar bill. She looked around and saw that she was the only child to receive a used item—and used it most certainly was. In fact, it was quite unusable.

Mae was as angry as Rita was disappointed when her daughter came home with a battered Yo-Yo for a Christmas gift.

"My mother blew her stack!" Mother Angelica recalls. "She marched me out to that old Packard, drove like thunder to the rectory and really let them have it. She withdrew me on the spot from St. Anthony. In minutes it was all over."

Afterward Rita began to understand what had really happened to her.

Why had she been ignored not only by her teachers but also by her peers? Was it really because she could afford only one dollar on tithe day? Or could it perhaps be something deeper, more profound? It was the divorce, she concluded.

Sure, they were poor. But poverty alone didn't explain the way people had treated her and Mae. Divorce was the explanation. Divorce was the unforgivable sin. It was the mark they wore like a scarlet letter, the emblem that caused boundaries to be drawn around every relationship. Divorce explained the rejection that Rita had sensed but could not describe or define. Now she felt as if everyone else had known something that she hadn't.

Remembering this time of sad realization is painful for Mother Mary Angelica.

"When it began to sink into my head that we were being

discriminated against because my mother had been divorced, I was absolutely crushed. I think I knew it for a lot longer subconsciously than I ever dared acknowledge on a conscious level. The rejection was truly overwhelming. It cut me to the very depths of my being. Divorce back then," Mother points out, "was practically the worst sin a person could commit. It just wasn't done, especially if you were Catholic, which of course we were. We were stigmatized, almost shunned. I was treated differently by teachers and had virtually no real friends."

In her desire to establish relationships Rita saved her nickels and dimes to treat classmates to movies. Being treated was a novelty—and social barriers or no, kids simply had a hard time refusing. Rita was never invited by anyone to anything. So she went on the offensive and asked others to go with her.

For a few hours she had all the friends she could want, at ten cents a head, surrounding her at the local movie theater. She prayed the movies wouldn't end so soon. As the grainy, flickering, black-and-white images gave way to the closing credits she was like Cinderella at midnight. Alone. Her "friends" simply vanished without a "thank you" or even a "see you later." Alone again.

"When I look back now," Mother says, "I recall this as a time of immense sadness. I honestly can't recall having a real childhood. There were no Christmas trees, no dolls, no friends. One week in the dry-cleaning business we made nearly ninety dollars and we just sat down and cried—in those days it was like a thousand! It was too good to be true."

When the pain seemed unbearable, a "wondrous grace," as Mother Angelica calls it, would suddenly and unpredictably burst forth like a ray of sunlight on a stormy day.

On one such evening, Rita was walking downtown, caught up in her own thoughts and oblivious to everything around her. She has forgotten where she was going, but she remembers beginning to cross a busy street, then hearing a woman's shrill scream behind her. She looked back expecting to see a woman in trouble and saw instead the headlights of a car bearing down on her with great speed.

With no time to get out of the way, she instinctively shut her eyes and waited for the fatal impact. A moment later she blinked and looked around her in disbelief. She was standing on a sidewalk! She felt as though two strong hands had somehow lifted her to safety.

A crowd gathered around. They had fully expected to see the limp, crumpled body of a child. It appeared to them as though she had been hurled aside by the careening vehicle. Instead they found a healthy, but quite frightened, little girl.

A busdriver who witnessed the event later reported to Mae, with some incredulity, exactly what he had seen. Rita, he insisted, had jumped or somehow been catapulted high into the air, easily clearing the onrushing auto in what seemed an impossible maneuver. He was profoundly amazed by the event.

As soon as she got home, Rita shared her story with her mother. Mae told her she'd had a premonition that something threatening would confront her young daughter that day. Mae's fervent prayers for her safety had miraculously been answered.

It was a grace—an extraordinary, wondrous grace—from a caring God who, Mae surmised, had definite plans for her daughter's future. Why else, she asked herself, would God have so spectacularly intervened to spare this child? Together mother and daughter offered thanks to God for His loving mercy. Rita and Mae would draw upon this rare moment of joy in the days of doubts and difficulties ahead. They had a new sense of purpose in life.

Rita was pondering all these things as she drove home that stifling summer evening in 1938. Life had certainly provided a series of setbacks. But quiet desperation had begun to give way to hope as Rita sensed within her the kind of confidence that can only be born of adversity. That confidence, marked

by resilient, aggressive vitality, became the sustaining force
that would carry mother and daughter through the troubled
years as they walked their own via dolorosa, the road of sorrows.

Rita pulled her car to a stop outside their aging apartment
building and girded herself to face her mother with another
fistful of accounts receivable. As she opened the car door, a
stabbing pain coursed through her abdomen. The pain came
more frequently now and with growing severity. She uttered
a silent, urgent prayer.

CHAPTER TWO

———— * ————

Crossroad

High-school years, as everyone knows, are terribly important in our lives. The decisions we make in our teens, the friendships that we develop and the way we come to view our world are critical to the formation of our adult selves. For so many high-school days are the ''good old days'' filled with fond memories and nostalgia—the time when we came of age. Not so for Rita Rizzo.

When she enrolled in McKinley High School, she and Mae were no more comfortable at home. Rather, their living conditions had significantly deteriorated.

Mae and Rita were frequently hungry and cold in the bitter Ohio winters. They continued to scrape a substandard level of existence from their faltering dry-cleaning business. Life was unrelentingly hard and there appeared to be no relief in sight.

''And the rats!'' Mother Angelica exclaims. ''We had sewer rats in our apartment this long,'' she remembers, waving two index fingers in the air to accentuate the claim. ''Those awful things would literally eat their way through our floors and we could hear them gnawing and scurrying across the room as Mother and I hugged each other in the middle of the night we were so scared. In the morning we would inspect the damage. It was really quite frightening.''

Mother Angelica succinctly describes her high-school social life in one word: "disastrous." She had no time to make friends, do homework or dream dreams. She does not remember having ever dated young men. "No time for 'em," she says. As she grew older and more independent, she became a true loner. Mae, ever more dependent, became demanding and possessive.

"She was a good mother, as good as she could be under the circumstances, which were quite adverse," Mother recalls, apologizing for Mae. "And I must say," she continued, "my mother loved me—I always knew she loved me. In spite of all the difficulties, I'll always remember and appreciate that."

While St. Francis of Assisi, raised in an affluent family, eagerly embraced the simple life, personifying it as his "Lady Poverty," Rita had no choice. At times there was not enough food in the house to sustain both Rita and Mae. On many occasions Rita gave her portion to her mother, pretending she had eaten at her grandmother's house. Her shoes were worn until they fell apart.

"I can remember stuffing pieces of cardboard into the holes in my shoes so my mother wouldn't know they were worn out," Mother chuckles. But cardboard doesn't hold up in the snow, and Rita trudged through more than three miles of it to get to school.

On one such bitterly cold morning Rita arrived at school after class had begun. She had started late. The snow had slowed her pace. She tiptoed into her economics class well into the lecture. The teacher was directing stinging criticism toward the class about their poor academic performance.

"Many of you have the ability to go far beyond what I see handed in to me in the way of homework," Mrs. Thompson accused. "And I know one person here who could be an 'A' student in economics if she would only apply herself and discipline her study habits," she challenged, looking straight at Rita who suddenly flushed hot in embarrassment and anger.

"I would like to see that person after class," Mrs. Thompson demanded. Rita's heart raced.

As the bell rang at the top of the hour, she slumped in her chair while the other students filed out of the classroom, some taunting her with derisive facial expressions. As the class outcast, she felt they were always eager to get their digs in. Mrs. Thompson closed the door of the classroom and walked slowly toward Rita, her head bowed thoughtfully, hands clasped studiously behind her. Removing her glasses slowly, she sat down beside her and remained silent long enough to make Rita squirm.

"Rita, you're a very bright young lady. You have tremendous potential, I can readily see that. You are just not measuring up to your abilities. I know you could be at the head of this class easily and . . ."

"I don't really care to be at the head of this class," Rita interrupted tersely. "I don't like you—I don't like people!" she blurted out, momentarily surprising even herself.

"That's your problem, Rita."

"That's my choice!" she shot back without hesitation. She stared at her teacher in defiance, expecting some kind of punishment. Instead, Mrs. Thompson slowly stood up, grabbed her briefcase and walked out of the room, leaving Rita alone with her own angry thoughts and her stomach ache. The pain was getting steadily worse.

"That outburst was all just part of my own childish defense mechanism, I can see that now," Mother Angelica recounts. "I was reacting to the rejection and the circumstances of my rather bleak existence at that time. I was being obnoxious in my feeble attempts to cry out for some kind of help."

In the midst of the pain and darkness, bright spots did, on occasion, emerge to shed light and warmth into Mae and Rita's lives.

There was, for example, the most extraordinary occasion of Rita's earlier miraculous escape from what seemed like certain death by a speeding automobile and for which they remained extremely thankful to God. Things had somehow changed since that day in spite of continuing, even worsening, hardships. They had an increasing sense that, regardless of circumstances, a court of last resort—a higher source of power—would meet their most critical needs. They were beginning to possess a very special faith in a power beyond themselves. Although they attended Mass infrequently, both nevertheless felt deep reverence toward God.

Rita began to find strength and solace in reading the scriptures, primarily the Psalms. They spoke of the majesty of God, the wonders of His creation and provided practical pearls of wisdom for living her daily life. She found them comforting. Most of all, however, she identified with David's soulful cries to God for deliverance from his enemies. She allowed these words to provide courage and strength in the face of overwhelming odds.

In her own way, Mae had also made a commitment to God. She refused to remarry, seeing this as a moral impossibility while her husband yet lived, even though remarriage would have given them financial stability.

"I can remember a number of quite eligible men coming to our little storefront dry-cleaning shop to visit my mother," Mother Angelica says, "but she would simply not consider remarriage based on her understanding of church teaching. This was her way of honoring God sacrificially. And, I must say, this was quite a commitment for her, particularly since she really loved one special man and would liked to have married him. But she said no." In this way, Mae was saying yes to God.

✻

Recognizing that the dry-cleaning business was a dead-end proposition, Mae decided that what she really needed was a change in work. Rita agreed, urging her to look at alternatives that could carry more promise. She needed a new job in a new environment—one that would better provide for them. But there seemed little chance of finding that job.

Late on the evening of January 31, 1940, Mae wrote these thoughts, a prayer of faith, in her diary:

> Dear Lord: tonight I pray to you. I don't even have the words, but you know my heart. Give me a position in life where I can be a light to you. Give me, oh Lord, a chance in life to be of some benefit. Penniless, Lord, I can do nothing. We need food and we must have clothing. We must eat and pay our bills. Lord, when you see fit to grant my prayers, grant me wisdom and knowledge. Open my mind. Give me hope. Give me the faith of a child and let me be your light, shining in the presence of my superiors. I have the feeling, Lord, that you have a surprise awaiting me. Thank you, dear Jesus, and good night. Your Mae.

Rita had become quite the optimist by age sixteen. She began to search for work on her mother's behalf, and she stumbled upon an opportunity that seemed overflowing with possibilities.

Rita was a politically precocious teen-ager and she saw some opportunities upon which she knew she could capitalize. Mindful of her mother's donated hard labor on behalf of the Republican party, and aware that City Hall was under the administration of Republican leadership, she approached the mayor's sister and boldly requested a job for Mae.

"My mother is a hard worker and has experience in the Republican party and business," Rita insisted. "She would make a good staff person, I just know it! Could you help my mother?" She felt a little like the biblical Esther, the young woman going before the king on behalf of her own family. She was nervous but confident that those in power would see things her way. After all, what did she have to lose?

"Here's what you should do," the mayor's sister said. "Have your mother write to the county executive committee—here is the address—and tell her to submit an application as soon as possible. I'm not going to promise anything, but I think she'll have a good chance at a job," she said, understating her influence considerably.

Soon Mae's prayer was answered. A letter summoned her to appear at City Hall for a job interview. She later learned the job was hers. The unfamiliar sounds of celebration filled their little house. Mae and her aggressive young daughter rejoiced at God's kindness.

*

Rita's stomach pains, which had begun to increase steadily in April of 1939, were so severe by 1941 she could keep the secret no longer. She had to go to a doctor. X-rays taken in November of 1941 showed alarming abnormalities in her stomach and intestines. Something was definitely very wrong, the doctors concluded. They found that Rita was suffering from a severe calcium deficiency. But a more specific diagnosis eluded her physicians. Together, Mae and Rita sought God for help. They had, after all, come to trust Him based on their increasing faith.

Mae returned late one evening from the office to find Rita in bed, crying from her ceaseless abdominal pain. "Mother!" Rita exclaimed through her tears, "I was worried you wouldn't come home. My stomach is getting worse and . . ."

"Just a minute, I have something to tell you," Mae interrupted with uncharacteristic enthusiasm. "It's something like I've never heard before in my life and I want you to listen. It is about a woman named Rhoda Wise."

Mae told an intriguing tale of a local woman who had been miraculously healed by Jesus under the most extraordinary circumstances imaginable. Rhoda lived not far away on Harrisburg Road. In 1932, at the age of forty-four, Rhoda had a large intestinal tumor removed. The operation led to severe complications four years later. Further operations in 1938 and 1939 to remove abscessed scar tissue led to wounds that refused to heal properly. During her long stay in a Catholic hospital, Rhoda, a Protestant, became interested in the rosary and asked one of the Sisters to teach her how to say it. She felt irresistibly drawn to Catholicism and sought instruction from Monsignor Habig, pastor of St. Peter's Catholic Church.

On June 1, 1939, she was received into the church by Monsignor Habig. In February, to her great distress, doctors informed Rhoda that she had terminal cancer. She checked out of the hospital on May 8 to die in her own home.

Later that month, in the early morning hours, she said Jesus appeared in her bedroom. She was startled and amazed by the appearance which was repeated again on June 28, during which time she was miraculously healed of her fatal condition. Relatives, friends and medical authorities were incredulous at first but rejoiced as they examined her abdomen. The large, open wound that would not heal had disappeared. Rhoda Wise laid much of her healing to the intercession of St. Thérèse, who accompanied Christ during one of the apparitions. (Known as the Little Flower, Saint Thérèse, who lived between 1873 and 1897, is the patroness of missions. She is also known for her simplicity and commitment to honoring Christ by doing simple, ordinary things in her Carmelite convent in Lisieux, France. She is often pictured scrubbing the convent laundry.) Rhoda Wise was certainly an ordinary person but one who had reportedly undergone a series of quite extraordinary events of divine proportions.

What particularly interested Rita, as she listened to the story, was the report of the stigmata—the visible wounds of Christ—plainly visible to all on Mrs. Wise's body. The marks were similar to those of St. Francis of Assisi, one of Rita's favorite saints.

At the end of her story, Mae paused to catch her breath, then turned to Rita. "I was thinking we should go to Mrs. Wise's home and ask her to pray for you," she said. "Perhaps God will use her to help you."

"Let's go!" Rita said. She was ready for anything that would alleviate her of the chronic pain.

Looking back today, Mother Angelica sees this as a pivotal time in her life—a crossroad experience for both her and Mae.

"I remember that time as though it were yesterday," she reports. "It was Friday, January 8, 1943. Physically, I was really at the end of my rope and I saw this as my last hope. The doctors didn't really seem to be able to do anything. I was a bit skeptical as we entered Mrs. Wise's house, but her warm, congenial manner put us at ease immediately. I can't put into words the feelings that swept over me as I entered the room where Jesus appeared to Mrs. Wise. It was awesome— that's the only way I can describe it. We weren't there more than thirty minutes, altogether.

"Mrs. Wise gave me a prayer to recite, asking the intercession of St. Thérèse which, of course, I read with all the faith had in me. I promised that, if healed, I would share with others this devotion to the Little Flower. We left the house that night with high expectations although my abdominal pain was as severe as ever and this caused me some concern.

"But we prayed the novena, which is nine days of prayer, and at the end of that time, on Sunday, January 17, something began to happen. I experienced deep misgivings and doubts about the entire episode and was tempted to forget the whole thing. I went to bed. In the middle of the night I suffered the worst stomach pain ever in one, brief moment. It was if I had been turned inside out. That morning, I got up and prepared to go to the 11:30 A.M. Mass. It was Sunday. Then, my heart skipped a beat! I suddenly realized that there was no pain whatsoever in my stomach. It was as if there had never been a problem! I walked around the house, almost in a daze, unbelieving. I was healed. There was absolutely no question about it. From that day till this, I have had no stomach pain. God had indeed performed a miracle in my life.''

Mother Angelica traces her lifelong commitment to God to this experience.

''Unquestionably, that was the day I found God and really began to pray in an entirely new way. It was the first time I really recognized God's active role in my life.''

Mae was also profoundly affected by this event. For the first time she sensed that God had a personal love for her. She was filled with faith and immediately began to share it with others. She was a truly changed woman. But she did have one concern: Rita's sudden, radical transformation had begun to frighten her.

Rita began to pray at every opportunity and took on an otherworldly demeanor. Being thankful to God was one thing, but Rita seemed to have gone over the edge. Mae was alarmed. Frequently, upon returning home from work, Mae would find her daughter praying in their shared bedroom, oblivious to her surroundings, oblivious even to her own mother.

''I'm a little concerned,'' Mae confided to her mother, Mary. ''I awoke in the middle of the night and Rita was not in bed. I immediately got up to find her and there she was, on her knees, at an altar she had erected. She was in deep prayer.''

The elderly Mary placed her hand on her daughter's shoulder. She gazed deeply into Mae's eyes. ''Mae, Rita doesn't belong to us anymore. She belongs to the Lord.''

Mae sobbed.

CHAPTER THREE

———————— ✳ ————————

Sister Mary Angelica
of the Annunciation

It was apparent to all who knew Rita, particularly her mother and grandmother, that her life was changing in a profound way.

The roots of this spiritual process lay in her unusual healing. God had apparently been working through subtle circumstances over a period of years, slowly building Rita's faith until she was ready for the full revelation of His love through the healing. When God did touch her in such a miraculous way, after years of pain and rejection, she was overwhelmed.

"You know, to be an outcast and suddenly have God single me out for preferential treatment was a dramatic role reversal for me," Mother Angelica explains. "I fell in love with God and really began to thirst after Him. My life was changed from that point on."

In the spring of 1941, when Rita graduated from Canton's McKinley High School, World War II was moving into full swing. Women flooded the job market, including Rita, who found a position in the advertising department of Timkin Roller Bearing Company in 1942. A workplace veteran, she deftly handled her new responsibilities and impressed her superiors.

While Rita was busy earning a living, her heart was nonetheless committed to the God who had made Himself known to her through His "amazing grace." After work, she went to St. Anthony's Church and prayed the stations of the cross. While many Catholics reserved this devotional prayer for the Lenten season, Rita made it a daily discipline.

She strongly identified with the trials Christ had suffered as He labored under the cross on which He would yield up His spirit. The pain that Rita felt, and which Jesus endured on her behalf, was lightened by the certainty of resurrection. In the stations of the cross, Rita prayerfully traced her own stumblings and misfortune and offered them up to God in exchange for inner renewal and strength.

Rita also attended Mass at every opportunity. Increasingly, she prayed to the Virgin Mary to intercede with Jesus on her behalf. She was inspired and comforted by the Holy Mother's courage in saying yes to God as her role in our redemption was put before her.

One warm evening in the summer of 1944, Rita Rizzo entered the darkened sanctuary of the Italian ghetto church, as was her daily custom. She dipped her fingers into the holy water, crossed herself and walked down the aisle toward the front of the church. Slipping into a pew, she knelt before the Blessed Sacrament, drinking in the silent wonder of Christ's special presence. A candle flickered in the darkness, casting dancing shadows across the painted statue of the Madonna on the wall to her right. Bowing her head, she began to pray to Jesus.

A thought began to materialize in the midst of her meditation: "It was like a simple fact—as if I had the unquestioning knowledge that I was to be a nun," Mother reflects more than four decades later. "What? A nun? I couldn't believe it! I didn't like nuns at all. In fact, I hated them. They seemed so strict and angry—I had a real problem with those people, and yet I knew I was to become one of them."

What irony! Rita Rizzo, who had become the virtual head

of her household as a child, was about to enter the cloistered world of quiet prayer and total submission to authority. Such a call could have come only from God.

She was at once excited and terrified. This decision would affect not only her life, but also the lives of others. The greatest obstacle in her path would be her own mother, who had become so dependent upon her. Mother simply won't have it, she whispered to herself.

Her thoughts raced. What were the ramifications of such a move? Her hands clenched in prayer, Rita asked God to guide her. The conviction that she should seek a vocation as a Sister was strong. She breathed deeply and released her burden to the Lord. As she stood gazing silently at the figure of Mary, tears welled up in her eyes. Monsignor Habig will have some answers for me, she concluded. He will show me the way!

Rita carried her secret for days until she had the chance to approach her pastor. Her decision to investigate religious life did not surprise him. Since he had observed Rita's transformation, he had almost expected the conversation they had as they sat together in his office.

"I believe God wants me to be a nun," Rita began abruptly. "I feel like He is calling me to religious life and, well, Monsignor, I need some guidance in making my choice." The secret was out. She relaxed in her chair.

Leaning toward the young woman, Monsignor Habig had the slightest hint of a smile on his lips. He studied her silently a moment.

"Rita, I think that's wonderful!" He grinned, gently grasping her hand. "I have seen God working in your life and I have observed your response with great interest. Like our Blessed Mother, Rita, you are saying yes to God. You are being obedient to His special call." He paused, thoughtfully. "Perhaps you should look into the Josephite Sisters in Buffalo. I would be happy to recommend you."

"Thank you, Monsignor. There's one problem—my

mother. I haven't told her of my plans. She'll be crushed when she finds out about this. I'm all she has and . . ."

"Don't worry, Rita. This is just between you, me and the Lord, okay? You keep me posted on how things are going." He accompanied her outside to the sidewalk, continuing to comfort and encourage her. Rita's head was bowed thoughtfully as she walked away. "I'll be praying for you, Rita!" Monsignor Habig called after her.

Rita was afraid to reveal her plans to Mae. There was no question about what her mother's response would be. They had lived through so much together. The blow to Mae would be heavy. Would she ever recover? Rita had, over the years, come to understand and accept her mother's emotional attachment to her, which made her decision more difficult.

She carefully planned her escape. Mae and Rita were sitting at dinner, thankful that the weekend was upon them after a hot summer work week. Rita toyed with her fork. "Mother, I am spending the weekend with Kathy O'Conner," she said as casually as she could. "She invited me."

Any other mother might consider this a normal weekend plan between girl friends. Mae knew something unusual was happening because her adult daughter had *never* spent the night away from home. This was a significant departure from the established routine. Mae was suspicious but she accepted Rita's story.

On Friday evening, Rita took a bus to Buffalo. She was, at least for the time being, protecting her mother from an emotional upheaval. While at the Josephite convent, Rita explored every angle of religious life with the nuns. They seemed kind enough and were open and accepting—a welcome surprise to one who had developed such a jaded view of nuns through her parochial-school experience.

While Rita was conversing with nuns, Kathy O'Conner's phone was ringing.

"Kathy? This is Mae Rizzo, Rita's mother. May I speak with her please?"

"Oh, hello Mrs. Rizzo!" Kathy's heart skipped a beat. She had to buy some time to think. What would she say? How could she keep Rita's secret? "How are you, Mrs. Rizzo? Rita has told me a lot about you."

"Is Rita there?" Mae persisted.

"Well, she stepped out for a few minutes, Mrs. Rizzo. She should be back any time. Can I have her call you?"

Mae knew something was wrong. "Tell me the truth, Kathy. Did Rita stay with you last night?"

The awkward silence was followed by Kathy's sigh. "Mrs. Rizzo, Rita went to Buffalo, but she will be back today or tomorrow, I'm sure of that."

"Why Buffalo?" Mae's voice cracked with anxiety.

"I'm not really sure, maybe she has a friend there or . . ."

"C'mon, Kathy."

"Mrs. Rizzo, Rita went to a convent. She is visiting the Josephite Sisters. She is thinking about joining," Kathy confessed, feeling she was betraying her friend. "She was afraid you would be upset so she said she would be here for the weekend. I'm sorry, Mrs. Rizzo, really!"

"So am I, Kathy!" Mae hung up, anger rising to the flash point. "How dare she do this!" she barked through her tears. "How could she leave me?"

When Rita returned to the home they shared with her grandmother, she had not yet removed her key from the lock before Mae exploded in a fury.

"How could you do this to me!" she demanded. "I can't believe you would do such a thing without at least talking to me about it first." Mae's wrath subsided into sobs. Rita was speechless. She should have known her mother would somehow find out. Now her search for a religious order would be much tougher.

While the Josephite Sisters accepted Rita as a potential postulant, they shared with her their frank opinion. She seemed better suited to be a candidate for a more contemplative order. Rita appreciated the honest evaluation and returned to Monsignor Habig for counsel.

"Rita," he advised, "upon further reflection, I agree with the Josephite Sisters. You really are a contemplative and I think I have a very good lead for you. I want you to visit St. Paul's Shrine of Perpetual Adoration. It's a Franciscan cloistered contemplative order located in Cleveland."

Rita was determined to continue her search. But once again she believed she had to take the path of least resistance by surreptitiously investigating the Cleveland-based order, hoping once again to minimize Mae's reaction. She borrowed money from her boss at Timkin Roller Bearing Company. He also allowed her to take a day off to travel to Cleveland.

She would be gone and back before her mother suspected anything. This time the plan worked. Rita visited the monastery and returned without creating a ripple at home.

She was impressed by what she had observed while visiting the Franciscan Sisters in Cleveland. It seemed strangely like home and she couldn't wait to return. Once the monastery communicated to her that she should enter on August 15, she began to make detailed plans.

Again, she borrowed bus ticket money from her cooperative boss who also promised to mail a special delivery letter to Mae after Rita arrived in Cleveland. Thus she resigned from her job and moved the sixty miles to St. Paul's Shrine.

*

Mae opened the letter with trembling hands. Of course she recognized the handwriting. She knew immediately that Rita had left home. She read the message as she slowly paced the room.

August 14, 1944

Dearest Mother,

When you receive this letter I will be in Cleveland. I have entered the Adoration Monastery at 40th and Euclid. You know it better as St. Paul's Shrine. This, my dearest Mother, I realize is a shock for you. But if I were to ask your permission you would not have granted it. To have entered in this way has hurt me tremendously. I wanted you to give me to our Lord as His spouse. It may be difficult for you to understand, but this is His will.

You have done many wonderful things for our Lord since my cure. He has a work for you to do. There are many souls that you can lead back into the fold. Your work is on the outside, winning souls for Him. Heed His plan and give generously without reserve to His most Sacred Heart. Because I will be His spouse, His love for you will increase greatly. He loves you very much and asks this sacrifice of you. He wants to be first in your heart. You have put me before Him. In the past, our Lord has tried to make you understand this. Do not, my dearest Mother, attach yourself to anyone or anything on earth but attach yourself to God alone, who is patiently waiting for your love.

A cloister, my Mother, is heaven on earth. There will I tell Him with every breath I take that I love Him.

Something happened to me after my cure. What it was, I don't know. I fell completely in love with our Lord. To live in the world for the past nineteen months has been very difficult. I love you very much and I have not forgotten what you have done for me. Please trust Him. You can always write and you can see me once every two months. You will see me with the grate open. I will write once a month. We belong first to God, then to our parents. We are His children. I ask your blessing that I may reach the heights I desire. I love you very much. I want to thank Grandma for everything she has done for me. I love you.

Always yours,
Rita

Mae received the news as nothing less than a conspiracy of betrayal by her pastor and her own daughter. Somehow she was blind to the spiritual enormity of Rita's decision to give herself totally to the service of Christ. She felt anger and rejection unmatched since her divorce. Wailing as if she were a mother who had lost her only child to an untimely death, she would not be consoled.

As the hours passed, Mae's sense of loss gave way to panic. She ran from the house to her parish church, seeking the pastor. Enraged, she accused him of arranging Rita's escape behind her back.

"The two people closest to me!" Mae shrieked hysterically. "You and Rita! Now she's gone and I can't even trust you. How could you keep this from me? How?"

The priest, having remained silent during her outburst, slowly rose from his chair. He looked at her kindly. "Mae, I'm sorry you feel this way but Rita is a grown woman and I felt her decision had to remain her own. She asked me not to tell you, so her plans remained confidential. I hope some day you will understand." He reached out to Mae but she turned away in tears. "Rita belongs to the Lord, now, Mae. You should be proud of her and pray for her."

"I'm all alone."

"We're never alone. Besides, you still have your own dear mother," the priest reassured her.

It was true, but somehow her mother did not compensate for the absence of her only child and best friend. She felt confused and guilty for reacting against a decision that obviously demonstrated Rita's supreme commitment to God. Suddenly she realized the focus of her anger was God Himself.

*

Any doubt that Rita had about her decision dissipated when the Sisters shut the large enclosure door behind her as she entered Cleveland's Adoration Monastery. A tremendous sense of reassurance surged through her spirit at that moment, fueling the flame of faith that had been ignited upon her miraculous healing nearly two years before. She had finally arrived, she thought. Then she reminded herself that this was not only the end of one journey but the beginning of another lifelong pilgrimage. Now she was a postulant—one who seeks admission to a religious order. It would be a time of preliminary inquiry and adjustment. Should her postulancy go well, she would then become a novice. The novitiate is a time of probation in religious communities that precedes first profession of vows. Finally, if all goes well, Rita would take her solemn profession of vows. The process would take years to complete and no one entering those doors fueled by idealism and faith is assured of mastering that process.

Now free of worldly ties, Sister Rita joined the Franciscan Sisters in prayer, worship and hard work behind the traditional monastery grate that walled them off from the outside world. Nothing gave her cause for concern in the early months of her stay at the convent other than her knowledge of Mae's agony over her absence and the unexplained and somewhat painful swelling which had begun to afflict both of her knees. This, of course, made prayer and genuflection painful, but she would not betray even a hint of discomfort. She had come too far to turn back.

Rita tackled her humble work assignments with obedience and enthusiasm. She worked in the laundry, baked altar breads for use in the Mass, labored in the kitchen and cleaned floors.

Sometimes, as she scrubbed on her hands and knees, she must have been reminded of St. Thérèse of Lisieux and her inspiring commitment to the mundane duties in life. Surely she drew strength from the example of St. Thérèse and recalled the saint's healing intercession on her behalf during her health crisis. Rita knew she would need those prayers once again as she worked with the painful, swollen knees that caused her daily discomfort.

Not only had her inflamed knee joints become an impediment to her required work assignments, but her spiritual commitments had also been compromised in the eyes of her superiors. She could no longer kneel or genuflect before the Blessed Sacrament. While she longed to make her vows, the community had come to doubt her vocation. Her normal six-month postulancy was extended to fifteen months. Even with this concession, everyone in the community wondered if Rita could make it—everyone except Rita herself.

She prayed to the Lord remembering that pain had once before drawn her closer to God. She asked God to use this affliction for His glory and the furtherance of His will.

Shortly after receiving the postulant's veil, Sister Rita received unexpected word from her superior, Mother Agnes, that a visitor awaited her. She had heard of her grandmother's death and suspected that Mae, who refused to visit, might send someone to bring her home. Rita seated herself in the visitors' quarters and the curtain was drawn aside. Through the cloister grille she recognized her uncle.

"Hello, Uncle Nick," Rita whispered.

The totality of his niece's involvement with the Sisters hit him as he peered at the veiled figure through the cloister bars. Overwhelmed, he choked back tears, unable to make the speech he'd been sent to make.

He returned to Canton defeated in his attempt to persuade Rita to reconsider. She was irretrievable now, he reported to his grieving sister, Mae.

Mother Agnes, the perceptive abbess of the monastery, invited Mae to attend a convent ceremony hoping to reconcile

mother and daughter. She could see Rita's pain at being separated from Mae. It was time, she reasoned, for healing to
take place.

Her intuition was right. On the appointed date, Mae Rizzo
was warmly received by Mother Agnes at the parlor grate.
Together they talked at length about religious life, procedures
within the convent and the nature of God's call to contemplative prayer. Mae softened. For the first time she began to see
the significance of her daughter's call to the convent.

"And Mae," Mother Agnes concluded, "Rita will, as you
know, have an investment ceremony here at the convent to
which you are, of course, invited. I would like to offer you the
privilege of choosing Sister Rita's new name. It is customary
to change one's name as she enters the order. From the moment of the investment ceremony, she will be known by that
name."

Mae wanted to embrace Mother Agnes but could not—an
iron grate separated them. Anxious to see her daughter for the
first time in months, she walked to the convent visitors' room
where she was left alone to greet Rita.

The time had finally come for their meeting. Mae and Rita
could see each other but were separated by the double grille.
The silence was filled with emotion. They wept, laughed and
conversed together at length. Their hearts and minds were
finally joined—reconciled in the knowledge that God's will
was, indeed, being done.

In the Adoration Monastery Sister Rita and her mother
began a new relationship, which neither would fully compre-
hend until much later. God, it seemed, had a special plan in
mind. It would be revealed in His own time.

That evening Mae Rizzo wrote a letter to God in her diary:

April 20, 1945.
To the King of Kings in the most Blessed Sacrament:
Today, I offer you my beloved daughter on her twenty-

second birthday. I give to you gladly today that which you had placed in my care. I have tried to raise her as I thought best. Forgive me, Dear Lord, for the offenses I have committed against you. I thank you for the deep wound you have placed in my heart. I beg you to shower many graces and blessings upon Rita all the days of her life and over those you have chosen to have charge over her.

I humbly beg to receive only the crumbs, for I know that you love me. I humbly ask for the grace of loving you more and more and the grace of winning souls for you.

On November 8, 1945, Mae loaded a bundle of gayly wrapped gifts and a beautifully decorated cake into her car and drove to Cleveland for Rita's investment ceremony. It was to be, quite literally, Rita Rizzo's wedding day—a marriage made in heaven—to Jesus. The ceremony is an ancient church tradition symbolizing the beginning of an eternal commitment to Christ within the religious community. It was Rita's transition to the novitiate.

Though Mae had come a long way in giving up her daughter to the convent, she was still ambivalent. She was reconciled to Rita, but she was reticent about her daughter's religious ambitions. She sat through the ceremony of investiture, clutching a soggy handkerchief in her gloved hands.

Suddenly, Sister Rita Rizzo appeared behind the altar grille in a white wedding gown. She was beautiful. Mae's sister-in-law, Rose, had created a stunning dress from the materials so carefully selected by Mae and Rita. And now Sister Rita seemed to glow as she wore it as a sign of her commitment to God. As the ceremony proceeded, Rita was taken out and dressed in another garment that symbolized her death to the world. Finally, she received the brown Franciscan habit and white veil of the novice.

Mae wept quietly during the Mass, barely able to participate in the liturgy. The memories of their struggle for survival
together over the years recalled for Mae the enduring cama-
raderie with which they had faced life's challenges. Her
daughter was taken from her, and she realized she could turn
only to Christ—the one with whom she had previously con-
tended for the loyalty of her child. Yes, her consolation would
be in the Lord—and in the joy she would have in bestowing
her daughter with a new name.

"Dear Sister," the presiding bishop finally intoned, "you
shall no longer be known as Rita Antoinette Rizzo. Your new
name in religion shall be Sister Mary Angelica of the Annunciation. You belong to the Lord now. God be with you."

On the evening of her investment ceremony, Sister Angelica
wrote an emotion-filled letter to her mother:

My Dearest Mother,

Today the greatest possible honor has been bestowed
on you and me. To have me marry an earthly king would
have been an honor but to be espoused to the King of
Kings is an honor that even the angels cannot understand.

We still have to wait until eternity dawns for both of
us to realize what it means. So many souls in the world,
much better than I, He might have chosen but His eyes
rested on you and me.

It is as if He were walking through a field of beautiful
flowers looking, and passing many beautiful ones by, suddenly picking a small one, weak and hardly able to hold
up its head. He walks away having made His choice. It
must be because there is no one on earth that needs Him
more than we do. We need Him every moment of the
day.

Let us then spend the rest of our lives in thanking,
praising and loving Him. Shall any sacrifice be too hard
for us whom He ever holds in His arms?

Shall we not be filled with spiritual joy, knowing the loving eyes of God rest upon us?

May my sweet spouse keep you ever close to His Sacred Heart. There is no loneliness for one who realizes His sweet presence.

I want to thank you once more for bringing me into the world, for taking such good care of me, for your *many sacrifices,* for all your love and devotion. Thank you for everything. May I become worthy of such a mother.

I ask for your blessing on this our day of days that I may become what Jesus wants me to be.

Your loving child and spouse of Jesus,
Sister Mary Angelica

Sister Mary Angelica, now a novice, was one step closer to the day when her first vows were to be made. While she corresponded with her mother on a regular basis, visits were allowed only once each sixty days. Through their prayers and written communications, however, Mae and Sister Angelica grew closer to each other as they diligently sought to intensify their relationship with God.

An elderly Canton couple, Mr. and Mrs. O'Dea, approached Mother Agnes one day with an unexpected and intriguing offer. "Take our mansion and sprawling grounds, transform it into a Franciscan chapel for adoration and a monastery, and it's yours for the keeping."

Mother Agnes charged Mother Clare and Mother Luka, who served with her on the monastery council, with overseeing the renovations and the establishment of what would eventually become Sancta Clara Monastery. Mother Clare and Mother Luka were aware of Sister Angelica's increasing knee pain and offered her an option. They called her into the convent conference room.

"Sister Angelica, we would like to present something to you, a new start in a new monastery. We'll need hard workers like you," Mother Luka said. "It's highly unusual, as you know, for a Sister to be transferred back to her home town, but we feel that your health might benefit from a move to the new Canton monastery."

Sister Angelica had mixed emotions. But she took this offer as a sign from God that, indeed, she should be involved in helping to pioneer a new Franciscan venture in Canton. "Yes," she responded. "I'll go."

The two superiors were impressed with the young novice. She was aggressive, energetic, responsible and demonstrated a deep spiritual disposition. But as long as those knees presented a problem, they agreed, the jury was out on first vows. Canton would be the ultimate test of her vocational future.

Sister Mary Angelica of the Annunciation packed her few belongings and moved to Canton, ready to begin a new work for the Franciscan Nuns of Perpetual Adoration. She believed God had once again used physical pain to direct her path according to His will, for on the day of her departure from the Cleveland convent the swelling and pain in her knees vanished, never to return.

However, for her, pain had brought about a maturing process in God's mysterious, unfathomable ways. Pain had become for her a means of communicating with her crucified Jesus. Pain, in some form, was to become her constant companion.

CHAPTER FOUR

—————✳—————

Sancta Clara

The rigors of religious vocations are demanding, especially in a monastic setting. This is why a number of stages are involved in the process of becoming a Brother, Sister or priest. Each new ceremony brings the aspiring member another step closer to permanent, final vows. Of course there are dropouts along the way.

Because of her inflamed knees, Sister Angelica had been precariously close—closer than she knew—to being a forced dropout on health grounds. Her spectacular recovery, however, persuaded her superiors to reconsider. Sister Angelica never once thought of giving up.

Just prior to her arrival in Canton in 1946, she began a canonical year, a time of reflection, study, prayer and discernment. It was a year-long retreat. A novice must be convinced and, even more importantly, her superiors must be convinced, that she is truly called to the cloister. There would be no visits for twelve months, even from her mother. It was in this period of time that Sister Mary Angelica moved to Sancta Clara Monastery at 4200 North Market Avenue, her home for the next fifteen years.

While the Sisters moved into the building immediately, they had much planning and work to do before that building fulfilled the function of a monastery. Within days of moving in, they began laying plans for the residence, the grounds and structural additions to the existing mansion. One of the first projects was the chapel, the central focal point for their lives of perpetual adoration of the Blessed Sacrament.

While the chapel was being prepared, the seven Sisters attended daily Mass at nearby St. Peter's Church. This was a rare opportunity to be outside the cloister. The Sisters stared wide-eyed at the world around them—a world that they had sworn to forsake forever. Still, they enjoyed the outings that they knew would end upon completion of their own enclosed chapel. Each day they arrived at the church early, filed to the front near the sanctuary and filled the first row. They prayed silently before the exposed Host.

They did not deviate from this established pattern until, one morning, Sister Angelica heard a familiar cough behind her as she prayed. It was unmistakably—her mother! Until now, they had endured their painful separation without attempting to contact each other.

What to most would be the prospect of a pleasant encounter between family members after Mass, became a frightening thought to the novice as she knelt between two other nuns. Mother and daughter knew no contact could be permitted between them in the canonical year. The prohibition suddenly seemed cruel and harsh. Sister Angelica winced at the thought of leaving the church without embracing her mother or engaging her in conversation.

What will she do when she sees me, Sister Angelica asked herself anxiously. She planned contingencies in her mind for the end of Mass. Maybe she would not be seen—perhaps she could depart undetected in the midst of the other Sisters at the end of Mass. Why should something so simple become so threatening? Her agitation grew.

During the liturgy, which seemed to last forever, Sister Angelica reached a moment of inner serenity. I am the Lord's, she proclaimed to herself. I belong to Him. He will strengthen me for this moment!

As the liturgy concluded, Mae stood at the rear of the church clutching her rosary tightly and crossing herself. She looked wistfully across the sanctuary at the visiting nuns in their brown habits. Immediately she thought of her daughter. As the Sisters walked toward the rear of the church, Mae's eyes met Sister Angelica's. Trembling, Mae dropped to a sitting position. She waved timidly, tears streaming down her face. She fought back her rising impulse to rush toward her daughter.

Through their fleeting, visual embrace, both knew they were being called to offer up yet one more sacrifice to God. Sister Angelica turned away and hurried from the church, a lump swelling in her throat. Mae buried her face in her hands, weeping softly. She lifted her rosary to her lips and gently kissed the crucifix, abandoning herself to God's love. It is true, she thought to herself, God's ways are not our ways. He seemed to be calling her with a still, small voice—but she couldn't quite hear the words. She simply said yes to whatever God would have for her, even if it meant continued separation from Rita.

*

The old O'Dea home underwent many changes in a short time on its way to becoming the Sancta Clara Monastery. There was more than enough work to go around. Most of the heavy labor fell to the three youngest Sisters, among them two postulants and Sister Angelica. Full of initiative, Sister Angelica eagerly rose to the challenge of creating a religious-community environment through long hours of tedious planning, demanding manual labor and problem solving with construction crews.

The community met frequently to discuss building progress.

"The new chapel is nearly finished," Mother Mary Clare announced at one such meeting. "And the new wing is coming nicely as well." Huddled around architectural drawings, they were generally satisfied with the way things were shaping up.

"And have you seen Sister Angelica? What a bundle of energy!" remarked another.

"She handles those men like a veteran foreman." Laughter filled the room.

"I have my eye on that one," Mother Veronica said. "She has obvious leadership qualities, no question about it. She has a future in this order." The others agreed. This young woman tackled her work with a rare vengeance and won disagreements with the contractors. They didn't stand a chance in an argument with Sister Angelica. Mother Veronica took the young novice under her wing and grew to love her like a daughter in what was to become a lifelong relationship.

The primary spiritual devotion to which these nuns were called is the adoration of the Blessed Sacrament. Their lives revolved around prayer centered upon Jesus who is present in the consecrated host that was exposed in the new Sancta Clara Chapel. Perpetual adoration requires ceaseless prayer participation on a rotating schedule that was more than the limited number of Sisters could manage.

The abbess decided that lay people could supplement the Sisters' commitment to adoration in the chapel and help in attaining perpetual worship. Sister Angelica invited Mae to share in this level of community life. Sensing that this was a special call from God to honor Him in a new way, Mae readily responded.

Several nights a week Mae drove to Sancta Clara knowing that she could not yet see her daughter. She was drawn instead to the Blessed Sacrament—called to uplift, honor and worship Christ. She could hear the faint, inner voice summoning her to deeper levels of prayer and spiritual commitment.

While the conditions of the canonical year called for physical separation, Sister Angelica and Mae met mystically through their mutual prayers before the consecrated host. For the first time, Mae entered into the decision her daughter had made two years before in choosing to join the Franciscan order. In a small way, she felt like part of the community, even if for only a few hours a week.

After almost three years in the monastery, January 2, 1947, was the date selected by Sister Angelica's superiors for her first profession of vows. She would, on this special occasion, take vows of poverty, chastity and obedience. Continuing to express her religious vocation in terms of a spiritual marriage to Christ, she sent this invitation to her mother:

> To our dearest friend:
>
> Jesus, Son of the Most High, and Sister Mary Angelica, daughter of Mae Frances, who, being espoused on January 2, 1947, for all eternity, wish to express their gratitude for all the hard work, the time and money so unselfishly spent to make their wedding so glorious. Jesus has looked down on all your efforts and blessed you with many graces. The Spouse has asked her Bridegroom to fill you with His peace and consolation. As the royal couple continue to live their hidden life together, you may be sure that they will speak of you often, asking the angels of their guard to protect you from harm and to provide for all your spiritual and temporal needs. Enclosed is a piece of ribbon which has touched all the holy places in Jerusalem. Another gift the Bridegroom has for you, but that one He will keep for the day when you will see Him face to face.
>
> Your ever grateful and loving,
> Jesus and Angelica

Once again, Mae observed Sister Angelica's celebration. This time she was far more at ease with the choice her daughter had made in giving herself to a cloistered life of service to

God. With her first profession of vows, Sister Mary Angelica of the Annunciation moved yet another step closer to the ultimate commitment made in religious life: the solemn profession of vows.

Mother Angelica looks back on the occasion of her first vows with dismay. "That day was a disaster! I was terribly nervous. Everything went wrong. It snowed, so everyone was late, including the bishop. In fact, he was so wet and cold we had to dry out his coat, socks and shoes before the Mass! Then, as he placed the ring on my finger during the ceremony, it fell off. I was a wreck. But I made it somehow. I remember thinking, gee, God, I hope this isn't a sign of things to come!"

With each ceremony, Sister Angelica was more determined to proceed with her vocation. Any reservations about a life of cloistered, contemplative prayer had long since vanished. To be sure, it was not an easy life. On the contrary, it was an existence filled with physical and spiritual demands that required endurance, patience and high levels of personal discipline.

"Let me tell you what the greatest difficulty was for me," Mother Angelica reveals, looking back on her monastic beginnings. "Community. Living in community with the other Sisters was, of course, a blessing in many ways. That goes without saying. But it was also a constant time of testing for me. I would often say to myself, 'Angelica, you would do just fine as a hermit, all by yourself.' And it was true! I loved being alone. Life in the monastery, because of its restrictive, close quarters, accentuates already diverse personalities and idiosyncrasies. And this can exaggerate the normal conflicts that take place among people living in close quarters. A lot of times I was really on edge. I have to admit—I had a real struggle. I was very impatient. But I knew I had to conform, not only to the community, but to the image of Christ who calls us to love one another and to bear one another's burdens."

An added challenge, she notes, was the fact that she was an

only child, while the others in the community had survived their formative years in large families where they developed social coping skills. She was suddenly plunged into a large, tightly knit family—one sibling among many Sisters.

In the midst of such challenges, however, special relationships grew between the Sisters that would endure for a lifetime. One such friendship began in January of 1951, just days after a new postulant, Kathleen Meyers, arrived at Sancta Clara. Kathleen, from Louisville, Ohio, would later become Sister Raphael of Mary Immaculate. Currently, she serves as Mother Angelica's vicar and community archivist.

"I guess you could call me the monastery scribe. I keep a running history of everything," she laughs. In spite of an excellent parochial-school experience, Kathleen Meyers was hesitant about answering God's call to the cloister.

"I'll never forget when my sister—she's a year older than I—entered the Holy Humility of Mary Order and became a teaching Sister. I was absolutely crushed! It was like losing her, somehow," Sister Raphael recollects. "Later, when God began calling me to religious life, I tried to go about my life like anyone else—I had a job, I dated. But it all seemed to turn to dust. I went off and asked myself what life was all about. I knew there had to be more. For five years I battled the call to religious life. I suppose you could say I was sparring with God. In retrospect, I am frightened to think that I very nearly said no to Him. Ultimately, though, I gave in to what I knew was God's will for me and joined the Sisters at Sancta Clara in Canton on January 13, 1951."

Apprehensive and shy, Sister Raphael looked for a bright spot in the monastery as the enclosure doors locked behind her. She found it in Sister Angelica.

"I'll never forget the first words I heard her say," Sister Raphael remembers. "I was working as an extern Sister—one who does special work with the guests, errands and outside responsibilities, freeing the other nuns to live separated lives of prayer. I heard a joyful voice exclaim, 'Isn't God good?' I was a bit startled, having just delivered some food through the turntable to the cloistered nuns. 'You're the new postulant, aren't you? Isn't God good?' she exclaimed again to me from behind the grill. It didn't take me long to find out who this spirited Sister was, and though I could not see her I knew I had a special friend and mentor within the monastery.''

Yet it was some time before Sister Raphael merged with the Sisters and got to know Sister Angelica. Canon law decreed that the residence for novices be separated from the older community of nuns.

''As postulants, we dressed in black for one year, preparing to receive the habit. As novices, we received the brown Franciscan habit and white veil and studied the rule of the Franciscan order. It is only after this that first vows are made,'' Sister Raphael observes. In the spring of 1952, she became a novice under the guidance of novice mistress, Mother Veronica.

By this time, Sancta Clara had become an established religious community. The new wing was completed and the grounds were beautifully maintained with the original gardens carefully manicured. The old brick mansion was nestled in the midst of thick, towering maples. Formal, tree-lined gardens stretched toward an open pavilion, encompassed by a small forest of tall evergreen trees. The beautiful, serene environment was conducive to prayer and contemplation. The Sisters would frequently walk the grounds, seeking their own space for study and meditation.

''Not everything in the monastery was dark and somber,'' Sister Raphael assures. ''In the novitiate, we had our fair share of celebration and fun, too. On the anniversary of St. Francis and St. Clare, we would abandon all restraint and dash about decorating our living quarters with streamers of bright crepe paper, flowers and angel figures I had painted. We often put on a play and acted out the lives of these saints. At Christmastime, I painted angels and little children on the windows to brighten the monastery. We sang Christmas carols for the other Sisters and even built a snowman in the courtyard for those in the infirmary. Then there were holy days! Every holy day of obligation—Christmas, Easter, Pentecost, the Immaculate Conception—found us preparing special music and chants to celebrate at Mass. From Advent until Christmas the monastery took on a special atmosphere of anticipation of fulfillment as we prepared for our celebration of the birth of Jesus. Holy Week was a somber time as we sang the Gregorian chants. Easter was exhilarating with its exultant celebration, and Pentecost was a time of triumph as we celebrated the coming of the Holy Spirit. To mark these special occasions, we would get together with the other community Sisters for picnics in the woods, recreation or just singing songs.'' In those days the Sisters found this a means of achieving a healthy balance in the formal and relatively rigid structure of pre-Vatican II monastic life.

After four years of life in the religious community, Sister Angelica had fallen into a rhythm of study, prayer, meditation and work. It was spring, a season she loved, and she often walked the grounds of the monastery thinking about the solemn vows she would make in less than a year. One afternoon she returned from a garden stroll to find the Sisters looking for her.

"Sister Angelica, Mother Clare would like to see you," one Sister reported matter-of-factly. "She says you have a visitor waiting." Sister Angelica walked buoyantly to Mother Clare's office. Perhaps her mother had come to see her. She enjoyed their visits—one of the special joys of being in her home town.

"You wanted to see me, Mother Clare?"

"Yes, Sister, please sit down. You have a visitor—I have been looking for you."

"It's probably my mother—I'll go down and see her."

"It's not your mother, Sister Angelica. It's your father, John Rizzo."

The young nun was stunned at the announcement. How could this be, she wondered, uncertainty welling up inside. She was shaken. How could she handle the situation with grace? She thanked Mother Clare and disappeared down the hall. Her mind raced.

Pausing outside the visitors' room door, she straightened her habit and collected her thoughts. She took a deep breath, looked through the grill directly into his nervous, darting eyes. He was tall and thin—still a handsome man, but cowering slightly. His sister, Mary, was with him.

"Please, sit down," Sister Angelica said. She fought back tears. "Coffee or tea?" she offered.

"No, no thank you. I can't stay long, Rita. It's been a long time," he said, fighting to maintain his own composure. "Your Aunt Mary brought me to see you."

There was an awkward silence. The situation seemed only to worsen by the second. Rizzo was unable to look his daughter in the eye. Though he knew she had been a nun for years, he was unprepared to see her wearing the habit and veil.

He broke down into sobs, concealing his face with his hands. Sister Angelica noticed a ring on his finger. She concluded he had remarried. In fact, as she would later learn, he had married a much younger woman—a former classmate of hers. John Rizzo struggled to regain his composure.

"How is your mother?" he asked.

"She's fine. I see her regularly. She has a good job now. She takes care of herself. She has had a hard life. A very hard life . . ." Her voice trailed off.

Biting his lower lip, Rizzo stared silently.

"Rita, I want your mother to know I'm sorry. I've caused you both a lot of pain. I know that. Would you tell her that when you see her?"

"Yes, I'll tell her. I'll be seeing her again soon."

"Is there anything I can do for you, Rita? Anything I can bring you?" he asked.

"I have everything I need here, but thank you anyway. I appreciate the offer. Wait a minute, maybe I do need something," she said, grasping for any need she might have in order to offer her father an opportunity to give her something. "See this spot in my habit? I could use some dry-cleaning fluid—yes, that would be very helpful." She felt compassion for him. He was a broken man—she could see that. After all, she knew what rejection felt like and wished it on no one— not even an enemy.

"Rita—I would like to visit you again. That is, if you don't mind," her father ventured tentatively, rising to leave. "I don't live that far away and, well, I could come from time to time. I would really like to talk to you again." There was an urgency in his voice.

"You may come to see me again, but you will need to clear your visits with my superior, Mother Clare. As you probably know, there is a limited schedule for visitation."

A deep sadness came over her as she peered through the grill at her estranged father walking slowly away, shoulders stooped, head down.

John Rizzo, bearing a small gift, returned a second time to see his daughter. The cleaning fluid worked nicely, removing the troublesome little stain from Sister Angelica's garment. After the visit, she struggled with her father's request to return on occasion to see her. She wondered what her mother's response would be.

Several weeks later Sister Angelica knocked on Mother Clare's door. She needed help from her superior.

"Come in! Oh, Sister Angelica—please, come in. Judging from the look on your face it's serious." Mother Clare was impossible to evade.

"Well, yes, Reverend Mother. I'm in an extremely difficult

position. It's my mother. Actually it's my mother and my father. When I told my mother that my dad had come to visit, she blew up! And that was nothing compared to her response when she found out that he wanted to come back for more visits. She screamed. 'What?' she said. 'Give up what few visits we are allowed, so your father, who abandoned us, can come and see you? Never!' It didn't seem to matter to her that he had come to apologize.''

"Sister Angelica, your mother has been deeply wounded. She has scars that have not yet healed—they may never heal. After years of struggle and sacrifice, she undoubtedly feels threatened by your father's sudden intrusion into your lives and is offended by his desire to cut into your allotted visiting days.''

"What can I do about visits? I am only allowed one every two months.''

Mother Clare bowed her head thoughtfully, prayerfully. "Sister Angelica,'' she said after several silent moments, "you know you are called to the cloister. I cannot, therefore, make an exception by granting more visiting hours. And, all things considered, your father must, in my opinion, yield to your mother's sentiments at this point in your lives.''

Sister Angelica was relieved yet troubled that she would have to confront her father with the final decision that he could not return to see her. Mother Clare seemed to read her mind.

"I will handle it, Sister Angelica. I will write to your father and, in as gentle a way as possible, inform him of our decision in this matter.''

"Thank you, Mother.'' Sister Angelica said to the smiling Mother Clare. She was feeling torn inside—troubled in a way she had not experienced since early childhood. Once again, she found herself reliving the trauma that had split her family.

This time it was John Rizzo who would feel the stinging reality of being on the outside looking in. She knew he would be heartbroken by the letter. She prayed he would somehow understand the position she was in.

Six months later, without warning, Sister Angelica received news that her father was dead. He was stricken by a massive heart attack from which he did not recover. On October 29, 1952, he died in his hospital bed. Tearfully, Sister Angelica prayed for her father's soul.

January 2, 1953, was the day Sister Angelica made her solemn profession of vows. After more than seven years of cloistered, monastic life, she was ready to make final her commitment to God and her community in a special Mass celebrated by Monsignor Habig. He had observed Angelica's progress through the years and, as she prepared herself for this occasion, he was proud.

The outer, larger chapel was filled with relatives and friends while the inner, smaller chapel was reserved for the Sisters. Mae looked on from a front-row seat in the larger chapel, her eyes brimming with tears. But this time they were tears of joy, for she had finally come to terms with her daughter's vocation. She had finally released Rita to fulfill her destiny as a Franciscan nun.

She had finally released Rita to be Angelica.

As part of the ceremony, Sister Angelica lay on the floor, face down in the shape of a cross. Four Sisters held a black pall over her. It was, in a sense, a funeral Mass—a recognition that Rita had died and that Mary Angelica of the Annunciation had risen in her place, empowered by Christ to live a life of sacrifice, obedience and prayer. It was a celebration of death and resurrection.

"It was a beautiful occasion," Mother Angelica remembers, "but I was really a little mystified and confused by Monsignor Habig's homily. He spoke of Abraham, Sodom and Gomorrah. I thought, what is this? It doesn't seem to relate to my vows at all! In retrospect, though, I can see how prophetic it really was. Abraham asked God to spare the two wicked cities for the sake of what righteous people may have inhabited them. We see our ministry today as a statement of faith in a media world that is, in many ways, extremely bankrupt, morally. We are just a few Sisters who are taking on Sodom and Gomorrah, hopefully with faith like Abraham, to proclaim the good news,'' she says.

In November 1953, Sister Mary Raphael made her first profession of vows. She sought to develop her prayer discipline by reading the lives of the saints. With God's help she was determined to follow their example. ''Then suddenly,'' as Sister Raphael puts it, ''into my life bursts Sister Mary Angelica—free, happy and full of the love of Jesus. I was feeling overcome by the external rigidity of the religious life in the monastery. It was like a kind of bondage. I read, I prayed and, yet, I felt dry and somehow empty. I knew I had been led by the Lord to the community but somehow I needed clarity and spiritual renewal,'' she recalls.

''Sister Angelica was the answer to my prayers. She had been sent to the novices' residence to hold an eight-day retreat. We all knew she was special from the beginning. She seemed like someone who had endured a lot but had come through it with victorious confidence. She became our friend and mentor—our lives were changed after that week.''

Today, on occasion, Sister Raphael will dust off an old notebook and read her journal entries. Thinking back to the fall of '53, she remembers that first guided retreat at Sancta Clara. ''My first experience of Sister Angelica's spiritual guidance was a memorable one,'' she says. ''I had no vocabulary with which to describe what was really transpiring in my heart. I simply was not able to express myself. I sat entranced before Sister Angelica as she began to describe the humility of Jesus and the beauty of this God-man for whom we had given up all and whose life and love we were seeking to imitate. She made me realize that holiness is attained by following Him and that He loved me and wanted me to become His own. He was, in ways that I had not recognized, providing me with opportunities to walk in His footsteps. She showed all of us the deep love for Jesus that would enable us to hang on to our vocations. She had an incredible air of assurance and her advice, we knew, had come from years of testing. As she led discussion groups and prayer sessions, my fears dissolved and I was very aware of being placed in the hands of one experienced at her trade. I knew my soul would be handled with gentle care and strong determination and that the sufferings in my life had been allowed by God to bring me to this moment in time. We all caught her enthusiasm for our mutual vocation. She wrote these three resolutions for me, during that first week, which I still find highly relevant—I often read them from my notebook:

1. My one thought, the ruling force in my life, will be an ever-increasing love of Jesus by which each day I will attain another degree of union with Him.
2. To accomplish this, I will keep the eyes of my soul continually on Jesus, not in a forced way, but as one who lovingly looks upon a beloved object.
3. Virtue or fall, no matter, each will be an opportunity to sink deeper into the sanctuary where Jesus dwells alone and where we live together as if no one else existed in this world.

"As the days sped by, I realized I was happier than I ever knew I could be," Sister Raphael reflects. "I found myself in the midst of a spiritual renewal."

Sister Angelica took on the postulants and novices as a mother would. Her chief concern was their spiritual development. She parceled out the writings of St. John of the Cross,

St. Teresa of Avila, St. Paul of the Cross, St. Ignatius Loyola, St. Francis de Sales, St. Bernard of Clairvaux and the other masters of the spiritual life to the Sisters like a doctor writing prescriptions. She became, as one Sister would later put it, a "true, guiding light to our community. She made us really want to become saints."

She regularly taught from the scriptures, combining readings with her own life experiences to drive home her points. Sister Angelica, claimed the nuns who received her teaching and encouragement at Sancta Clara, possessed a wisdom and insight beyond her years.

"We all had the sense that Sister Angelica had been through many trials and heartaches that strengthened her resolve and leadership abilities. She was a spiritual giant to us," Sister Raphael says.

Although Mother Angelica winces at being labeled a supernun, she does believe that adverse circumstances and physical pain helped mature her.

"Those kinds of things will make you or break you. A lot of the outcome depends on your attitude—I really believe that! And, of course, there are the mysteries of God's graces operating in our lives which we must receive and appropriate," she says. "But it is the pain that has taught me most. I can barely remember a time in my life when I haven't had it in some form," she says, adding that she rarely takes any form of pain medication. "I think God uses it to get my attention, you know, like a two-by-four between the eyes!" she jokes, laughing merrily in spite of frequent discomforts.

"We were so terribly impressed with Sister's teaching and example," Sister Raphael relates, "that we hardly noticed her limp, which worsened over a period of time. And never once did we remember her talking about it. Only later did we learn that she had a congenital spinal defect that painfully affected her vertebrae and had been aggravated by a fall on a soapy floor."

*

One day her work assignment had been—what else—scrubbing floors in the tradition of St. Thérèse, the Little Flower. Modern technology had made the task easier via an electric scrubbing machine—which proved to be Sister Angelica's undoing. The large, unwieldy machine churned away with Sister at the helm. Suddenly, Sister Angelica lost her balance on the slick, soapy floor. She dropped to her knees and struggled to stand.

The scrubber careened out of control, and the large, spinning brushes scooped up the electrical cord. The machine spun into wild loops.

Sister Angelica tried to regain her footing and subdue the scrubber. Instead, the flying handle caught her across the chest and flung her, back first, against the wall. As she lay on the wet floor, temporarily stunned, she knew she was in trouble. Her spine had taken the full force of the blow and the pain was blinding. Somehow she managed to crawl across the room and jerk the plug from the wall. The gyrating cleaning equipment ground slowly to a halt. Sister Angelica forced herself to her knees and then her feet. She was able to walk, with great discomfort, in a stooped position.

In the following months, the injury produced more pain, but Sister Angelica went about her activities silently bearing that terrible burden. Finally, two years after the accident, she was hospitalized on orders from her superiors.

She was fitted with a body cast and given oversized crutches in the hope that natural spinal alignment would occur. It didn't. Six weeks of traction followed. Still no results. An operation was ordered.

On the evening before surgery, she answered a knock at her door. "Oh, come in, doctor, please," she said, motioning to him, the rosary she held flipping about at each wave of her hand. "Please sit down, if you have some time."

"I can only stay a moment, Sister. Tomorrow we operate— you know that. You should also know there is a fifty-fifty chance you will never walk again." Incredulous, Sister Angelica awaited something—anything—from the doctor to comfort her. "Good night, Sister." He turned and walked away.

She was panic-stricken. The pain she could live with, even though she was allergic to pain-killing drugs. But paralysis! That was more than she could bear. Tears dampened her pillow. It was a long, sleepless night of desperate, rambling thoughts and prayer. But sometime, in the early morning hours, she recalled the miraculous healing of her stomach.

"God!" she called out in the silence. "You didn't bring me this far just to lay me out on my back for life. Please, Lord Jesus, if you allow me to walk again I will build a monastery for your glory. And I will build in the South!" she declared knowing that the Bible Belt, Protestant South was hardly fertile ground for Catholic undertakings of that magnitude. Nonetheless, she made the promise.

Sister Angelica slowly emerged from an anesthetic fog. Disorientation gradually faded. She realized the operation was complete. As she propped herself up on her elbows, shooting pain racked her lower back. She peered down at her feet—two lumps under a white sheet. First the right foot—yes—it moved freely. She was elated. Now, the left foot. At first, there was no response. Then, a little movement. She was cautiously optimistic. Exhausted and dizzy, she fell into a deep sleep.

*

The Sisters cheered as Sister Angelica hobbled home with the help of a back brace, a leg brace and a crutch. Four months of hospitalization had ended. The nuns of Sancta Clara welcomed her back enthusiastically—especially those who had come to regard her as their spiritual director.

"Sister Angelica!" Sister Raphael laughed, "you are walking! God has answered our prayers." And so He had. Angelica waited for the right moment before telling anyone about her promise to God.

"We observed closely as Sister Angelica bravely struggled to walk," Sister Raphael recalls. "Sister Joseph and I vied with each other, attempting to make her more comfortable. She endured everything so cheerfully. All the Sisters who came to the monastery infirmary to cheer her spirits went away tremendously encouraged. It was a truly uplifting thing for us to see."

Sister Mary Angelica had a following of nuns who gravitated to her for spiritual direction and guidance. Paradoxically, her weakness had caused Sister Angelica to become a pillar of strength among her peers. She simply refused to let circumstances deter her from goals that included strong leadership in developing the monastery. She was gaining invaluable experience for what, in faith, she knew would be her mandate at some future time: building a monastery of her own.

During her long recovery process, Sister Angelica requested a meeting with Mother Clare. "Mother," she began with some hesitation. "I need to share something with you. I made a promise to God and, with your permission, I would like to carry it out."

"Yes, Sister Angelica, continue," Mother Clare urged.

"I told God that if I could walk after my operation I would build a monastery for Him in the South." Angelica waited for a reply, intently studying Mother Clare's expression, which wasn't promising.

Mother Clare, however doubtful she may have been about

the feasibility of such a plan, had long since learned not to underestimate Sister Angelica's ability to attain her goals. She replied carefully, encouraging the Sister without giving absolute approval. "Let's see to your health, first, Sister. When the time is right, we will pursue this matter further."

"Yes, Reverend Mother." Sister Angelica knew she was home free. It would only be a matter of time. She believed that, ultimately, she would get her way, not because of her own ambitious designs but because she believed this was God's will.

Recognizing her skills in the areas of spiritual leadership and financial planning, the Mothers of the community eventually elected Sister Angelica to the advisory council, for which she would earn the title of "Mother." She had become canonically what many of the Sisters had already come to regard her—as a council Mother. There was quiet, restrained excitement in the ranks.

As the months went by, Mother Angelica fought to regain her strength. By sheer determination she battled for mobility from bed, to wheelchair, to crutches, until only one crutch remained. Also, a leg brace would become a permanent fixture, requiring her to lift her left foot as she walked. The nuns were amazed at the swiftness with which she could hobble about. "What would she be like," one nun was overheard asking, "if she were in perfect health?"

With the approval of her Mother superior, Mother Angelica finally approached several Sisters with her vision for a new monastery.

"Our purpose must be to love Jesus and to grow in union with Him. We will be one family, sharing everything in common like the early friars around St. Francis. We will share with each other what the Lord is teaching us, growing together in a loving, caring atmosphere. I will choose the Sisters who will join me in this pilgrimage, training them and building a community living as a family. But," she hastened to add, "it will still be a truly monastic community."

Mother Angelica was ahead of her time. The new community she envisioned was revolutionary, unlike the traditional, tightly structured hierarchy. She dreamed of a religious group without the historical class distinctions. Her plans predated Vatican II monastic reforms by more than five years.

"I came to believe that excessive rigidity and structure tend to warp personalities," Mother Angelica comments frankly today. "We desired an environment that would nurture each Sister's relationship with God, enhancing her individual gifts to serve instead of regimenting them according to the traditional system. We were inspired by God toward a more family-like atmosphere. And we realized something about the South," she says. "We knew that in order to survive in a Baptist Belt environment, where monasteries were almost unheard of, some creative changes would have to be implemented. It was a gradual process of adapting. This really took years to accomplish."

Mother Angelica, in her desire to make good on a promise to God, reached toward the deep South. Little did she know that her reach would one day extend beyond the confines of the cloister—and far beyond the Southern regions of the country.

Rita Rizzo at age one and a half in 1924.

At seventeen, Rita worked hard helping her mother with the dry cleaning business when not going to school.

Bishop McFadden accepts Mother Angelica's vows on January 2, 1947.

Mother Angelica, with Mother Veronica, shows scale model of future monastery, Our Lady of Angels, to Archbishop Thomas Toolen, 1961.

As workmen lay the brick for EWTN's new studio in 1984, Mother Angelica reviews blueprints and tours the worksite.

The satellite dish.

The formal dedication of EWTN on August 15, 1981. In the wheel-chair is Sister Mary David, Mother Angelica's mother.

Mother Angelica in the TV studio.

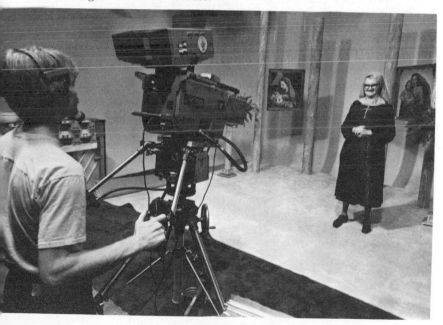

"Mother Angelica Live"—watched faithfully by millions each night.

With President Ronald Reagan
on Columbus Day, 1983.

With Cardinal Bernard Law,
Archbishop of Boston

With the Apostolic Delegate, Archbishop Pio Laghi.

Mother Angelica presents Pope John Paul II with a replica of the satellite dish.

Morley Safer interviews Mother Angelica on *60 Minutes*, June 1985.

CHAPTER FIVE

―――*―――

Our Lady of the Angels

The cold war was in full swing, Dwight D. Eisenhower was president of the United States and Elvis Presley was the rage of a new generation in mid-50's America. Although the nation was changing, timeless monastic traditions continued without interruption in the cloister of Sancta Clara Monastery. Mother Mary Angelica and the community of nuns in Canton awakened at 5:00 A.M., prayed the divine office, attended Mass, recited the rosary and, of course, prayed before the Blessed Sacrament. This was all balanced against rotating work schedules and other community assignments. While the routine was predictable, almost to the minute, the contemplative nuns would not have characterized their life-styles as boring. The tedium of the call to religious life was, in itself, part of the sacrifice willingly offered to God.

Some of the nuns of Sancta Clara, however, had another enterprise. Mother Angelica, Sister Raphael and Sister Joseph sensed God drawing them together for a very special purpose—starting the new monastery Mother Angelica had promised to God. And so they had begun to make plans. Some persons in high places, however, were indifferent toward their idea.

"You know, there were many who simply did not understand our contemplative vocation, even back then," Sister Raphael says. "Some people—even in the Roman Catholic leadership—would wonder why we weren't the kind of nuns who were teachers or nurses, doing something active for our vocational ministry. But to us, the calling was very special. We felt we were giving our entire lives directly to God through contemplation and adoration before the Blessed Sacrament. Our very being became our ministry, so to speak."

Sister Raphael speculates that this attitude may have been the root of the initial disinclination of authorities to grant permission for a new monastery.

"Of course we expected some delays and hangups in the entire process of getting permission for the project," Mother Angelica says. "We had to seek cooperation from our order, we had to write our bishop for a transfer and there were numerous lengthy procedures to take up with Rome. One hurdle, for example, was our ages. Sister Raphael had to be thirty-five to be a vicar and I had to be at least forty to be the abbess of a religious community, according to canon law. We were, by church regulations, underage for the task ahead of us; so special approval from the Vatican was required before we could even leave the cloister. Ultimately, we received the permission, but not without some stresses and strains. These things we handled through standard channels, expecting that it would take a significant amount of time, but what we definitely were not prepared for was outright rejection of the idea by our own bishop. Each time we wrote to him for approval he would find a reason to deny it. We were terribly disappointed, as you can imagine. We spent years on this before, finally, he wrote back granting us a provisional go ahead on the condition that we could find a way to support ourselves." Even now, Mother Angelica displays exasperation with the bureaucracy she encountered in attempting to launch her vision.

Before the permissions were granted and legalities were settled, Mother Angelica had begun dreaming of ways to raise the necessary funds for a self-supporting religious community of Sisters. This would require innovation, business sense and full use of the developing entrepreneurial skills that Mother Angelica knew she possessed.

"Earthworms!" she shouted one day as she thumbed through a magazine. Before her was an advertisement explaining how a business could be built raising live bait for fishermen. "We could grow our own worms and supply all the fishermen in the area! It will be our first fund-raising drive," she confided to Sisters Raphael and Joseph.

Together they took the idea to Reverend Mother Veronica, who had by then succeeded the late Mother Clare as abbess of Sancta Clara Monastery. Brimming with enthusiasm, Mother Angelica explained how, utilizing the monastery base ment, they could raise thousands of earthworms, marketing them as bait. "This will be the beginning of our program to fund the new monastery!" she said. "What do you think?"

Mother Veronica squirmed, images of giant night crawlers in the monastery filling her mind. "I appreciate your initiative, Mother Angelica, I really do. But, somehow this idea doesn't seem, well, very monastic." With that, Mother Veronica politely declined to lend her support to the earthworm marketing scheme. But Angelica was undaunted. After all, she thought, Mother Veronica's objection was not to the idea of raising funds in itself, but to the mode. Therefore, the right project would undoubtedly be accepted.

Soon, Mother Angelica was back in Mother Veronica's office for round two. "What about this idea, Mother?" she began. "We order the components of these fishing lures, assemble them and sell them to fishermen." She held up a photograph showing colorful, creative fishing lures that could be designed and made from kits. And just think, Mother Angelica reasoned to herself, the very word "fisherman" sounds so wonderfully apostolic! How can she say no to this?

"How much do you need to test this idea?" Mother Veronica finally asked cautiously, examining the picture closely.

"Five dollars," Mother Angelica replied without a moment's hesitation.

"Done," came the final word from the abbess. "Just keep me posted, Mother Angelica."

"Yes, Reverend Mother Veronica." Mother Angelica immediately shared the encouraging news with Sister Raphael and their other ally in the cause, Sister Joseph. That day they sent for the sample kit and waited with high expectations.

A fortnight later Mother Angelica, still hobbling with a crutch from the effects of her back problems, limped into Sister Raphael's room. "Sister Raphael!" she exclaimed in childlike glee, "Look! Here it is—the kit!"

"Oh, let's open it now!" Sister Raphael squealed, joining the festivity of the moment.

Together they scurried to Sister Joseph's room. Minutes later, all three bounded up the stairs to the laundry room to inspect their new fund-raising packet, whispering in hushed tones of anticipation. Mother Angelica unwrapped the box, spilling its shiny contents out on the table with a loud clatter. Inspecting an inventory of hooks, spoons, spinners and other paraphernalia, they wondered aloud how they could assemble the complicated-looking jumble of pieces.

"It's simple!" Mother Angelica interrupted. "We just design a couple, put them together and test them out in the bathtub." Laughter filled the room.

Soon the three eager nuns were busy assembling the lures in experimental configurations. Sister Raphael gingerly applied Band Aids to Mother Angelica and Sister Joseph. Punctured fingers were the price they would pay for experimentation with the razor-sharp hooks. Finally, filling a bathtub with water, they pulled their new creations just below the surface to observe their movements. Laughter and splashing could be heard in the halls of the supposedly silent Sancta Clara Monastery.

"Hey, I think these things will really work!" exclaimed Sister Joseph, the only nun in the group who had ever gone fishing.

The unity and commitment between the Sisters did not escape Mother Angelica's notice. There was more to this process than simply selling fishing equipment. She sensed a team coming together around this project, a team that would undoubtedly face mountain-sized obstacles. This was a preparation phase. Give me a couple more Sisters like these and we'll be downright dangerous, she chuckled to herself.

Later that week, Mother Angelica stared over the shoulder of a repairman who had come to the monastery to fix their malfunctioning refrigerator.

"Hey, Bill," she said. "Sister Raphael tells me you are a fisherman. In fact, I understand you are going fishing this weekend."

"That's right."

"I've got a hot tip for you, Bill!" Mother Angelica said.

"Yeah?"

"Yeah. Listen, you stay put and I'll go get something that might change your luck a little." Mother Angelica disappeared down the hallway to her room, returning with a small envelope. She dumped the shiny lures out on the kitchen counter. "Try these," she smiled. "And let me know how you do."

"Okay, Mother Angelica. By the way, where did you get these lures? I paid a buck and a half apiece for lures similar to these just last week."

"Just tell me how they work," she replied with the look of mischief in her smiling, dark eyes. She raced back to her room mentally calculating the profit potential in marketing lures. She had paid only five dollars for the entire box of lure components, and each one went for a dollar and a half in retail outlets. She could hardly contain herself. A few days later, Bill the repairman reported to Mother Angelica that he had experienced success with the lures.

"Mother, you should have seen these fish! I caught two that were this big—well, maybe they weren't quite that big. But they were big enough, that's for sure! Hey, Mother, you got any more of those lures? I could use a few more." He was ecstatic, and so was she.

Mother Angelica jumped into action immediately. With an assembly line in mind, she said, "Okay, Sisters, let's get on with it! Bill hauled in several fish with our lures, so it is time to crank out a few hundred of these things," she said.

Mother Veronica, still a little on the skeptical side, nevertheless authorized the funds required to purchase full kits of lure components from the factory. Mother Angelica ordered the raw materials and, in a matter of weeks, the Sisters were laboring over an entire new creation of fishing gadgets, christening their new business St. Peter's Fishing Lures.

With high hopes, borrowed funds and a rented mailing list of the names and addresses of 2,000 fishermen, Mother Angelica and the two Sisters launched their first direct-mail marketing campaign. They printed brochures, stuffed envelopes and shoved their bundle of mail through a turntable where the extern Sister delivered it to the mailman, but not before hauling their bag of letters into the monastery chapel for a special prayer session.

"Please, Lord, help us with this project. We commit the whole thing to you," Angelica prayed fervently.

"Mother lifted those letters up to Jesus and laid everything on the line," Sister Raphael recalls. "We expected miraculous results—we just knew that 1,999 fishermen from our list of 2,000 would immediately order our lures. You can imagine how our hearts sank when, after several weeks, only two men responded."

Mother Angelica was incredulous. "How could He do

this?'' she demanded one evening as she commiserated with Sisters Joseph and Raphael. ''After all, this was for God! We did it for Him. I can't even look up at Him when I go into the chapel, now.''

Sister Raphael shudders at the memory. ''Mother Angelica and Jesus were definitely not on speaking terms that week,'' she says.

But God, it would seem, was working at His own pace and in His own economy. One of the 2,000 letters found its way to a fisherman by the name of Dale Frances. He also happened to be the managing editor of *Our Sunday Visitor,* a well-known national Catholic newspaper. Frances was intrigued with the Sisters' story and immediately published a feature article in the paper about the nuns who were determined to build a monastery with fishing lures. Within days of publication, Mother Angelica and her lures were a coast-to-coast hit. Numerous other papers and periodicals also picked up on the story. It was a promoter's dream. And, apparently, she struck a responsive chord among fishermen.

''We were swamped with orders almost overnight—it was great fun!'' Mother Angelica grins. ''We ordered another load of lures and began naming them according to our special designs. There was Wit's End, Little Mike, St. Raphael, Habbakuk, St. Peter's Chains and others. They were all marketed under the umbrella name of St. Peter's Fishing Lures, and all of them were in demand.''

Widespread involvement by lay people in Mother Angelica's special projects had already become an hallmark of her vocational style and would continue to expand dramatically. Somehow she had the ability to draw interested supporters into the raw excitement of her plans for the future. Her enthusiasm was contagious. One Chicago fisherman, caught up in the excitement of Mother Angelica's dream, ordered one of each type of lure. He was a professional printer and helped the Sisters upgrade their sales program by designing and printing a beautiful promotional brochure. The four-color foldout gave a more professional look to the St. Peter's Fishing Lures business. The printer, John Padlo, completely surprised the nuns by sending them a large box full of brochures at no charge. More encouragement came from far and wide across the country.

"People didn't just rush to support me, or to support my project," Mother Angelica is careful to point out. "This thing was God's project and, really, they were supporting Him. I just happened to be in the middle of everything at the right time."

"That's generally true," other Sisters confirm, "but let's face it, without Mother Angelica's own special gifts of communicating with people, and without her forceful personality, these crazy, wonderful things just wouldn't happen. She is the clear, motivating force behind everything. Yes, God is in it, but God uses Mother in special and amazing ways."

St. Peter's Fishing Lures became the project on which the nuns began building a large, extended family across the nation who eagerly participated in building the future monastery. And God's providence became increasingly evident as the Sisters moved out in a strong faith commitment. At times, when things seemed hopeless, extraordinary events transpired.

"That first mailing had us running scared—we were in the hole, financially, and we were very disappointed that there wasn't more response," Mother Angelica explains. "But just look at what came out of one man taking an interest in our fishing lures. You know, the Bible doesn't tell us anything about the apostles catching fish on their own. But when they followed the commands of Jesus, they made a haul of fish that nearly sank their boat! On our own, we are really nothing. But with God, anything is possible and we began to learn those lessons back then." Mother Angelica easily slips into homilies based on lessons the Sisters have learned. "With God, you've got to be careful what you ask for—you just might get it!''

Sister Raphael recalls the time when some of the Sancta Clara nuns casually mentioned how nice it would be to have a grotto built around the statue of the Virgin Mary on their property. They wanted a place to pray and meditate outdoors on nice days.

"Of course Mother took it seriously and ran with it," Sister Raphael recalls. "She knew her grandfather had helped a number of Italian immigrants get started in their own restaurant business, so she called several of them up, explaining that she needed some assistance. 'How much money do you need, Mother?' they asked her, 'I don't want your money—I want you!' she told them. Not one refused. Those men formed a work crew and labored all summer until nightfall each day until the job was completed. Sometimes I think Mother would make a great politician! She really knows how to motivate people.''

The other Sisters of Sancta Clara were amazed. By autumn of that year, they had a beautiful grotto, masterfully constructed of large stones, concrete and a white, beautifully sculptured statue of the Blessed Mother. It was tucked in between towering shade trees and was attractively landscaped. At the end of the construction project the volunteer laborers tearfully thanked Mother Angelica for the privilege of participating together with her on this project. "It is our special monument to God and to the Virgin Mother," they proclaimed with pride.

"I'll pray and ask her to get you into heaven through the back door!" Mother joked. They all responded in a loud round of laughter.

*

As the years passed, Mother Mary Angelica became more steady on her feet, although she required an aluminum crutch to get around and, on occasion, she would use a wheelchair. Overall, however, she was regaining her strength and mobility. The exception to the healing trend occurred each winter when the cold weather would nearly always produce extreme back pain and muscle spasms. Although cold winter air frequently forced Mother Angelica to retire early in order to alleviate the pressure of standing and walking, she betrayed no hint to others of the agony she felt. To this day, the Sisters are amazed that she does not take pain-killing drugs.

"She hides the fact of her pain remarkably well," Sister Raphael says, "and she has her own way of dealing with it."

Indeed, Mother Angelica remains philosophical about the thorn in her flesh. "To me," she says, "pain is a treasure. I have become accustomed to pain. Of course, it becomes terribly difficult at times, but next to my vocation it has been the cause of many graces. I know that on my own I can accomplish nothing. Pain makes me dependent on God for everything. It keeps me with Jesus. It is a gift, a kind of security that keeps me from becoming proud and arrogant or from taking credit for what God is doing."

One particularly painful afternoon, Mother limped slowly to her room, feeling a sense of exasperation that the pain was getting the best of her. She collapsed on her bed with a sigh, carefully adjusting the position of her troublesome left leg. She breathed a prayer and closed her eyes, fully expecting to drift off to sleep. Instead, images began to materialize in her mind's eye—building designs. Her pulse quickened slightly and she suddenly sat up in bed, blinking. Still, the architectural shapes persisted in her imagination. She could see that they were plans for the new monastery.

Up until that moment, Mother Angelica had not really allowed herself to think in specific terms about the proposed monastery structure. Bishop Walsh's previously negative responses had been a temporary and disappointing impediment. Since the success of the fishing-lures project, however, he had relented and granted the Sisters the final permission to proceed. Mother Angelica sprang from bed, hurriedly laid out a sheet of graph paper and began sketching. Her drawings became the blueprints for what would one day become Our Lady of the Angels Monastery.

Everything seemed to be coming together quite well. A small group was forming, funds were accumulating in a fairly predictable cash flow and permissions had been granted. Then, to Mother Angelica's great frustration, another snag developed. As she presented her building plans to Mother Veronica, she was told that another nun in the monastery, with more seniority than she, had suddenly and rather forcefully expressed interest in building a new monastery of her own.

"What?" Mother Angelica gasped, trembling. "It's no secret that we had intentions of building a monastery."

"That's exactly it, Mother Angelica. Others found out and now they want to push their own plans. This is an extremely delicate situation for me to handle," Mother Veronica stated in grave tones. "But I believe I have found a way in which God's providence will determine the matter once and for all. You will need a bishop's written invitation to build a monastery in his diocese, you know that. You will both mail out letters of intent to two bishops on the same day. Whoever receives a positive response first will proceed actively with plans for a new foundation."

It was a Solomon-like approach to a thorny problem. The two mothers mailed letters to two bishops from one mailbox on the same day. Mother Angelica, Sister Raphael and Sister Joseph bridled just a bit in the knowledge that all of their efforts and dreams were riding on a single postage stamp and the permission of a bishop they didn't know.

"We prayed and agonized for three days," Sister Raphael says. "On the third day a letter came, addressed to Mother Angelica. We were almost afraid to open it when we saw the return address on the business envelope. It said "Archbishop's Office, Mobile-Birmingham Diocese."

Mother Angelica finally broke the seal, extracted the letter and read:

> Dear Mother Angelica,
>   Ya'll come!
> Sincerely,
> Archbishop Thomas Toolen

The Sisters laughed and cried. The decision was irrevocably made—now there would be no turning back.

"We should never have doubted," Sister Raphael says. "God was with us every step of the way. God has honored the central desire of Mother's heart—to love Jesus and make Him loved. That seems to be the reason He has used the weak to confound the strong, as the scriptures say. Our whole monastery apostolate is a witness to this truth."

Having overcome yet another obstacle, Mother Angelica immediately went to work on the architecture of the proposed monastery building. She used her sketches as plans to build a scale model. Meticulously, methodically, she fashioned a detailed cardboard representation of the layout, complete with electrical and plumbing plans. It was important to her that the archbishop receive this building concept favorably. Mother Angelica did not want to be stuck in a house converted to a temporary religious community building, as was so often the case with new foundations. She wanted to launch a vigorous new venture that would accommodate the growth she knew would be taking place in the future.

The plan worked perfectly. On her first visit to Archbishop Toolen's office, she hand carried her model monastery, guarding it like a mother hen. She was submissive in attitude but firm and straightforward about her wishes for the land and the building. She capped the meeting with cash-flow projections

based on fishing-lure sales and just happened to have a couple
of newspaper articles on their business venture for added per-
suasion.

Impressed by Mother Angelica's drive and ingenuity, Tool-
en approved the plan, suggesting that Mother begin research-
ing real estate at her earliest possible convenience. A victorious
Mother Angelica returned with the encouraging news to Sancta Clara. Shortly after her return, the southbound nuns were
even more elated to learn that the Sancta Clara Monastery
board had authorized a $5,000 grant toward a new building—
a hefty commitment to supplement the growing capital raised
from the fishing-lure project.

In the spring of 1961, Mother Angelica and Mother Veronica traveled to Alabama to look for a plot of land. Joined later
by Sister Joseph, the nuns combed the countryside for likely
prospects. They were taken in as guests by the Trinitarian
Sisters who displayed tremendous generosity to the temporarily homeless nuns from Sancta Clara. "We came for dinner
and stayed eight months!" Mother laughs, always thankful for
God's timely provision through other brothers and sisters in
the faith. Finally, after a strenuous search, a fifteen-acre parcel
was located in Irondale, a suburb of Birmingham. The price
tag: $13,000—the exact amount netted from the sale of the
fishing lures.

Mother Veronica returned to her responsibilities at the
Canton community while Mother Angelica and Sister Joseph
were left to pioneer the new monastery. They rented a little
house attached to the acreage and settled into overseeing the
building project. There would be much to do and they would
need all the help they could get, so a new member of the
community was being considered for acceptance. She would
keep house, cook and entertain guests. This would free the
others to tend to ongoing fund-raising endeavors and to the
oversight of the construction work.

The new Sister who would move down from Canton was

interested in perhaps becoming an extern Sister with the intention of permanently joining the cloistered life. They invited her to join them immediately. Her name was Mae Frances Rizzo.

In a turn of events that neither mother nor daughter could have predicted in their wildest speculations only a few years earlier, Angelica had become a Mother, Mae a Sister, together again in a religious family-community. Mae, in the years following Rita's investment as a nun, had softened toward religious life and deepened in her Catholic faith. God, in ways only He could have managed, had been subtly speaking to Mae, preparing her heart for the day when she would embrace Him in a cloister, following the example of her own daughter. As work teams began preparations for laying the foundation of the building, Mae arrived, joining her daughter—now her Mother superior—and Sister Joseph.

Officially, the groundbreaking ceremony for the new monastery took place on July 24, 1961. Archbishop Toolen presided over the happy event, heaving a shovel load of dirt through the air to signify new beginnings. Mother Angelica, Sister Joseph and a few close friends looked on in eager anticipation. Through visionary eyes, Mother could see the concrete, beams and roof all firmly in place. The actual process of building, however, would present opportunities for learning patience through the challenge of unexpected barriers.

Ignoring the architect's caution that the building site was dangerously uneven and sloping in one particular location, Mother Angelica pressed the construction crew to expedite the framing process. Gradually, however, it became apparent as the walls went up on the hillside that there was a large hole in the courtyard measuring fifty by sixty by twenty feet. One afternoon she walked with the architect to the problem area.

"Now do you see what I mean?" he asked in a I-told-you-so tone of voice. "You should have sold this land while you had the opportunity."

"No way!" the feisty Sister snapped back. "This is the place. We just need someone with a hill they don't need to fill in this hole." She was only half facetious.

"Sure," the architect replied sarcastically. "Simple as that." He wondered about the stubborn nun's intentions.

"It's up to God, that's all." She limped defiantly away on her ever-present aluminum crutch.

The following Saturday morning she reluctantly returned to the troublesome site and peered down into the rolling, bowl-shaped cavity. She stared silently for a long while, whispering a short, urgent prayer. Suddenly, she was aware of someone's presence just behind her.

"Yup. You've got a mighty big hole there," drawled an old man in denim overalls. He had a cheek bulging with tobacco and projected a stream of it squarely into the chasm.

Well, that's one way to fill it, Mother Angelica thought to herself, half wishing the eccentric onlooker would just go away.

"Yup. You need some dirt," he said finally after marching and spitting his way around the yawning hole.

"Yes, sir, I most certainly do," Mother replied, tempted to commend him for his grasp of the obvious, but she held her tongue.

The old man walked up to Mother Angelica, scratching the stubble on his lean, lined face and squinted at her for several seconds. "Y'know, I've got this hill in my backyard. Every time it rains the damn thing dumps a ton of water in my basement. You want it?"

"Yes! Yes! I want it!" Mother Angelica shrieked.

By Monday afternoon twenty truckloads of dirt had filled the hollow and Mother was once again cheering on the workmen.

"Let's get on with it, guys!" she said. It was a phrase she was becoming known for.

"It was amazing," Sister Raphael recounts. "Things would go wrong somehow and Mother would ask for the craziest things—and get them! It was as if God looked down and said 'Okay, Angelica. You asked for a hill. You've got it.' ''

Mother Angelica, by no means the helpless nun stereotype, impressed the work crew with her forthright leadership. Sister Raphael remembers an incident involving an electrician who made the mistake of underestimating the head nun.

"This gentleman barged into our command headquarters—the small house we were renting—and demanded to speak to the supervisor. 'I'm the supervisor,' Mother answered. 'I mean the contractor—give me the contractor,' he asked again. 'I am the contractor!' she replied. By this time the man was fidgeting and impatient. He slapped the building blueprints down on the kitchen table and said, 'Look. I need someone who can read these plans.' Mother put her hand on her hips, stared him in the eye and said, 'You're looking at her.' He unrolled the complicated-looking drawings and said with a smile, 'Okay, Sister. Check them.'

"Mother examined the complex jumble of lines and immediately placed her index finger on a specific electrical diagram. 'Look here. This is wrong. This outlet is definitely in the wrong place.' Lowering his head in disbelief, the wiring specialist scrutinized the layout. After a minute, he sheepishly admitted that she was right and quietly left, a bit embarrassed, I think. After that no one questioned Mother Angelica's authority to direct the construction process," Sister Raphael laughs.

As the monastery was being built, pictures and articles began appearing in local newspapers and the public began taking a genuine interest in this community of nuns in the making. Well-wishers came to the construction site with sacrificial commitments. One businessman donated all the blocks and concrete required in the monastery. Another gave his services to blast rock and move earth. Two women provided the bricks for the exterior facing from their family-owned brick yard. On top of this, eleven thousand square feet of high-quality floor tile and hundreds of gallons of paint were donated to the Sisters.

At one point, when funds for the heavy construction ran out half way into the project, Mother immediately went with a heavy heart to inform the crew that they could not proceed to work on the building. They unanimously voted to continue construction without pay until the project was complete, stating that they would receive their wages as Mother was able to pay. Shortly after completion of the work, a series of unexpected donations came in—just enough to pay off the workers for their labors.

Lesson by lesson, problem by problem, the Sisters finally finished their monastery. Elation replaced frustration and joy replaced disappointment as they looked upon their building— the building originally envisioned by Mother as she lay on her bed in pain. It was hard to believe that it was actually standing, it's gracefully sloping roof reaching for the sky like folded, praying hands.

On May 8, 1962, Mother Angelica returned to Canton for the final time. "It was really difficult, in a way," remarks Sister Raphael. "I had lived at Sancta Clara for eleven years and Mother Angelica had been there for fifteen years. It was a little frightening—like leaving the nest for the first time."

The Sisters prepared for a new phase of religious life. Mother Angelica, Sister Raphael, Sister Joseph, Sister Michael and Sister Assumpta loaded their few belongings into a donated station wagon and headed South. It was a happy but tearful time for all the Sisters because there was no assurance that the Irondale community would have any further personal contact with their dear friends at Sancta Clara with whom they had spent so many wonderful years.

On May 20, 1962, the Irondale, Alabama, community of Franciscan Nuns of Perpetual Adoration closed themselves behind their cloister doors. Our Lady of the Angels Monastery was formally dedicated to the Lord.

CHAPTER SIX

———✳———

Renewal

Building a new monastery in the South where only 2
percent of the population is Catholic was, to say the least, an
adventure in living by faith. It was a way of life Mother Angelica and the nuns of Our Lady of the Angels Monastery would
adopt permanently. They have always seen it as a life-style
that forces them to depend on God's provision and guidance,
somewhat like the children of Israel who found themselves in
the desert looking to the Lord for their daily sustenance. Indeed, Mother Angelica had become so caught up in complet-
ing and dedicating the monastery building project that she had
overlooked the realities of basic community needs—like the
need for food. But again, help was on the way—a surprise
delivery of manna from heaven.

Joe Bruno, a supermarket owner, took a personal interest
in the new monastery after hearing about Mother Angelica
through the local media. He drove to Irondale to tour the new
facility and was greatly impressed by what he saw. He wanted
to participate in a meaningful way with the Sisters in their
ministry.

"Mother Angelica," he said, "I want to make a special
commitment to you and to the monastery. I want to donate
all the food you will need for the first year of your operation."

Mother was dumbstruck at the offer, realizing she hadn't

even worked out a monthly grocery budget for the community. "Oh, Mr. Bruno, honestly, I'm terribly thankful but I don't know . . ."

"I insist. After all, I have a number of stores. It's the least I can do for your new venture." He wouldn't take no for an answer; food flowed in abundance to the community. At the end of the twelve-month period of time, Mother Angelica called the generous grocer to express her gratitude for his invaluable assistance.

"You're most welcome, Mother Angelica. I am honored to have helped you out—but let me tell you something more," he responded. "As long as I have a supermarket, you and the Sisters will always have food. You've got my word on that!"

Sister Raphael remembers this act of generosity that came at a pivotal time in the early days of the monastery. "You know, that was really a godsend to us," she says. "Like so many other blessings, it was a surprise out of the blue. And God took care of Joe Bruno too. When we moved to Irondale he had thirteen supermarkets. Now, he has more than five times that number and fifty drugstores on top of that. Someone recently asked him if he was still feeding the Franciscan nuns. He replied by saying that he couldn't afford not to!"

As important as food is and as thankful as the Sisters were to be the recipients of such a significant gift, they still had many financial obligations that had accumulated in the building of the monastery. The dust of the construction had barely settled when bills began to roll in at a sobering rate. Full of faith and enthusiasm, the nuns of Our Lady of the Angels had been just a bit oblivious to the balance sheet. They were quickly brought down to earth with a resounding thud when the final tally of accounts payable showed a total of more than $90,000.

"It seemed like such a large amount of money. And remember, this was the early 60's before high inflation hit the economy. It was a little scary, but you know, it made us depend on God. From the very beginning we had to look to Him for everything," Mother Angelica points out. "It's amazing to see how He has authenticated and confirmed our original commitment through His timely provision. And He keeps stretching our faith—as soon as we would learn one lesson, along came another and the stakes were usually higher than before."

Through the generosity of supporters in the Birmingham area, the debt was paid off in five years, allowing Mother Angelica to set her sights on bigger challenges for the monastery. It seemed to those who really knew her that Mother could not be fulfilled outside of a weighty, pressing challenge from without, as well as within, the religious community. It was in the heat of battle that she rose to her highest level of vitality.

When Mother Angelica decided to build a monastery, she was committed to the concept of laboring on more than just beams, bricks and mortar. Just as the church is not merely a building, but a living body of believers in Christ, a monastery is a living, breathing entity composed of persons given to Christ in prayer, meditation and penitential living. This living element of the monastic life must be nurtured and built by the abbess of the community. Among Mother Angelica's goals was the spiritual development of the Sisters under her care. From the beginning of the new community, Mother invested substantial energy into this endeavor on a daily basis.

"Mother gave us a lesson every morning after breakfast," Sister Raphael says. "It was a time when she would teach and share with us her ideals for our monastic life together. Her primary thought was that each of us should become holy as individuals. She was totally committed to this idea."

Mother could see that her "raw materials" were of very high quality indeed and, that given the time, she could build a strong group of Sisters who would somehow have an impact on the world for God. By late summer of 1962 there were seven Sisters living at the monastery, including Mother Angelica.

On May 20, Mother Angelica's natural mother, Mae, became the community's first postulant. She went on to receive her habit at her investment ceremony on January 2, 1963, and made her first profession of vows exactly one year later. Mae and Mother Angelica had come full circle and were together again, bringing their dynamic relationship into the family of Sisters. Mae became Sister Mary David of the Infant Jesus and would spend the rest of her life in the monastery, functioning as an extern Sister at first. In a monastic sense, Mae, now Sister David, would become a daughter. Her daughter, Mother Angelica, became her Mother.

Then there was Sister Veronica, who brought with her a tremendous backlog of experience. Born Charlotte Hardy in Detroit in 1893, she worked for General Motors and entered religious life at the age of thirty-eight after a long-held desire to become a nun. Entering St. Paul's Shrine in Cleveland, she met Rita Rizzo and observed her transformation into Mother Angelica.

In 1946 she went with Sister Angelica into Sancta Clara and later spent two years in Washington, D.C., helping to found the Adoration Monastery. She returned to the Canton monastery as a Mother vicar and novice mistress, ultimately to become abbess. Her grasp of the history of the order and individual Sisters would become a valuable asset to the Irondale Monastery where she still lives today. When asked what she considers Mother Angelica's greatest strength to be, she simply replies, "telling things as they really are!" While she expresses amazement at how often her abbess has made the right decisions when confronted with difficult choices, she nevertheless frets a bit at the enormity of the financial commitments made by the monastery in its media projects.

Sister Raphael's role had been one of importance from the beginning. Mother knew she could be totally dependent on her vicar for support and follow through in managing the affairs of the community. She sensed in Sister Raphael a kindred spirit—an agreement that together they could make a tremendous difference in the hurting world around them.

Sister Mary Joseph was born Elizabeth Olson, one year before Mother Angelica. On February 3, 1950, she entered religious life at Sancta Clara Monastery where she first met her future abbess. With a sharp, inquisitive mind and numerous other skills going for her, she was a natural choice for pioneering the new monastery in Alabama. She would become a pillar in the community.

Mary McManus entered religious life and became Sister Mary Assumpta, and like the others, moved down from the Canton community, eager to establish a meaningful work for the Lord.

Evelyn Shinosky, from Warren, Ohio, would take the name Sister Mary Michael at Sancta Clara and would become the youngest founding member of the new Irondale community. Somewhat shy and reserved, Sister Michael had a profound commitment to the order's primary mandate of perpetual adoration. Her loyalty to the church, her love for the Eucharist, and her talents were to make her a valuable member of the community.

Mother Angelica surveyed her group one morning during a lesson and concluded that each one possessed the gifts needed to make the monastery function successfully.

"Each one of you is special," Mother affirmed in one of her morning teaching sessions. "You are unique. Each of you has the potential of becoming a saint. But remember, you can't do it by trying to be someone else. You can't show me one saint in the history of the church that imitated another saint to become holy. You must be yourself imitating Christ—not someone else imitating Christ." She paused, looking at each Sister in turn, making each one feel she was the sole object of her instruction. "You won't find in the Bible where

Jesus remade His apostles. He didn't shake His finger at Peter and say, 'Okay, Peter, you're impulsive and blustering, you must become someone else.' Absolutely not! Our divine Lord used what He found in their individual natures and worked from that point. He used grace to build on nature.''

The new abbess observed the Sisters' responses, sensing she was sending the right signals. Clearly, she was in control, but not in a dictatorial sense. ''It's easy to talk about having a family spirit—it's easy to talk about treating each other as mature individuals. But we must learn to actually do it—to respect the ideas and opinions of others when they are contrary to our own. We must realize the tremendous importance of each Sister, chosen by God as a spouse of Christ, that she carries Jesus in her soul. The way we treat another Sister is the way we treat Jesus. This, ultimately, will determine the quality of our relationship with Him.''

The Sisters were inspired and encouraged by Mother Angelica's words and by her leadership. Each one felt totally indispensable to the success of their mission together. Each was empowered by Mother Angelica's words of wisdom to know God and then make Him known. She would instruct them extemporaneously, as the Spirit led, without notes or books, from her own spiritual wealth of experience. Drawing on the strengths she had acquired through difficult times, she led the Sisters by word and example.

''We have been amazed at how Mother maintains her zeal—her intensity,'' reports Sister Joseph. ''And as important as her teaching has been, it is her own life—her own example of faithfulness to God and the gospel—that continues to impress us all.''

Sister Raphael agrees. ''It's Mother's own spirituality that inspires us all to keep striving for holiness. And her unique teaching on the lives of the saints encouraged us to see God in our individuality,'' she adds.

Indeed, Mother Angelica had carefully selected stories taken from the lives of Catholicism's greatest heroes of faith, sharing them with the Sisters daily. She was especially fond of repeating tales of those who were somehow ahead of their time or whose uniqueness created difficulties for them, sensing that the Sisters would need preparation in this area. She strengthened them for the possibility of suffering, yet expounded on the need for joy in their lives.

"Remember now," she was frequently heard to say, "joy is the mark of a Franciscan. Real joy is not contingent upon the circumstances. It is not affected by poverty, pain or any kind of hardship. We find it in the little things around us—a gift from another Sister, the beauty of an early morning sunrise, the rain, a letter. True Christian joy is constant."

"It's really incredible how many different lessons Mother could derive from the lives of the saints. There's still no end to it," Sister Raphael observes. "Where she gets it all, I really don't know."

"It's true, the lives of the saints are so inspirational—that's why I've always referred to them. They are examples to us all. But I'll tell you something," Mother Angelica laughs, "the people who wrote about their lives ought to spend forty years apiece in purgatory for making them all seem so perfect! These people were human beings with faults and shortcomings like all of us. We need to hear more about their humanity, their frailties, their fallibility. This in itself should encourage us all, that in spite of our problems and our limitations, we can be holy people. I think that's an exciting idea. So, yes, the lives of the saints are inspiring. There is no question about that, but they weren't perfect beings wearing halos around!"

Mother Angelica was, in many respects, walking a very thin line when it came to directing monastic life at Our Lady of the Angels. She was attempting to teach the Sisters to think for themselves, yet she was operating a religious community founded on principles and rules of canon law. She was seeking ways to generate funds for the monastery without upsetting the delicate balance of the call to the cloister. And she was spearheading a distinctly Catholic work in a distinctly non-Catholic region.

Some of the weight was lifted from her shoulders when, in the mid-60's, the Second Vatican Council reformed religious life in many ways. The revised rules allowed for more structural freedom and a major increase in the level of interaction that religious community members could have with the outside world. The Vatican II "Decree on the Appropriate Renewal of Religious Life" (*Perfectae Caritatis,* October 28, 1965) discussed the evangelical counsels, better known as the vows of poverty, chastity and obedience, and called for a renewal that would adapt religious communities to modern times. A 1969 document, "Instruction on the Contemplative Life and on the Enclosure of Nuns" (*Venite in Luogo Appartato,* August 15, 1969) dealt more specifically with areas of monastic reform that affected the Our Lady of the Angels community. It is important to realize, the document said, that we can be in the world and yet not be of the world. The enclosure would continue, but new conditions would allow for modifications and modernization. When the official changes came down to the diocesan level, Our Lady of the Angels Monastery was more than ready to implement them. As usual, Mother was ahead of schedule.

"We just knew we had to modernize," Sister Raphael says. "Not only was there a tremendous need to bring the church into the twentieth century, but in Alabama, we needed to become more relevant to the world around us if we were to carry on with our mission."

The Second Vatican Council was notable for the profound and extensive reforms that would alter Catholic life from liturgy to evangelization. Among other things, the church wanted to make the gospel more relevant to the world at large. One means of doing this was to utilize more aggressively the mass media to spread the good news.

One such document was the "Decree on the Instruments of Social Communication"(*Inter Mirifica,* December 4, 1963), which dealt extensively with communications and the church's use of modern means to propagate the faith. A subsequent document, "Pastoral Instruction on the Means of Social Communication" (*Communio et Progressio,* January 29, 1971), further clarified the task at hand. Through modern technology, the world had become a much smaller place in which to transmit ideas. The Council had embarked upon bold new initiatives designed to capitalize on all means at hand to communicate its message.

This was of special interest to Mother Angelica and to the other Sisters because of their desire to "love God and make Him loved," as Sister Raphael puts it. Obviously, they were loving God in their perpetual adoration before the Blessed Sacrament and in their radical commitment to prayer, which could amount to over five hours a day. The rest was more difficult. It meant somehow communicating their love of God to a waiting world in order to make Him loved.

"Mother's wheels were always turning," Sister Michael says. "She was always thinking of ways to accomplish something big. After building the monastery, we just knew she would have to sink her teeth into something more—another challenge for God."

But first it was imperative that the community establish itself on a firm foundation. Mother and the Sisters began to fine-tune their business ventures in order to ensure the cash flow needed to sustain their operational needs. One change, for example, was the discontinuation of St. Peter's Fishing Lures because, as Mother puts it, "those Southern fish just weren't biting on Yankee lures!"

The Sisters, after considering their marketing options, went from fishing lures to peanuts. After preliminary research, they purchased the equipment to roast, package and ship peanuts to retail outlets. It was an immediate success. Football stadiums, race tracks and independent concession stands sold roasted peanuts from Our Lady of the Angels Monastery. The business lasted two years before it ran into a terminal snag. A businessman involved in transactions with the monastery and with retailers demanded a kickback based on quantities of peanuts sold through his channels.

"Mother just said 'no way' and that was that," Sister Raphael states. "She said flatly that we weren't about to sell our souls over peanuts! We sold the equipment and shut down the business. At that point, we made a major decision. We decided that from then on we would just trust in God for all of our needs. From that day to this, He has provided for us in every way."

This was a watershed experience for the community—subtle but highly significant. No longer would commercial projects be engaged in simply to meet material monastery needs. If there was work to be done, reasoned Mother Angelica, it must be more centrally related to the mission of the church. And that, as she saw it, must be communicating the gospel.

Mother and the Sisters prayed, seeking guidance for the future of their community as they continued to fulfill their order's call to a cloistered life of prayer and adoration. There remained a sense of excitement and anticipation. Where, they all wondered, would God lead them? How would He use them to communicate His love through their little group?

As the 60's came to a close, the community, which by now had begun to add slowly to its number, had firmly established itself as an entity in the small Birmingham suburb of Irondale. Built on the strong foundations of the gospel, monastic tradition and Mother Angelica's unwavering vision, it was definitely there to stay.

By the summer of 1970, it was apparent that the winds of the Holy Spirit were blowing through the Christian world in the form of the charismatic renewal. Both Catholic and Protestant churches were experiencing a new power and dynamism that emerged in a movement in the late 60's. Although the nuns of Our Lady of the Angels Monastery had heard rustlings of these happenings, they were not directly in contact with them until a certain young Josephite priest happened upon the scene. The priest appeared one day at the monastery as the Sisters were working in the hot sun landscaping the front of their property.

"Here we were, wearing our straw hats to shield us from sunburn and aprons to protect our habits, moving dirt and rocks for our grotto and foundation project," Mother recalls, "and this young priest drives up in his air-conditioned car to go to pray in our air-conditioned chapel. Then he approaches me and says, 'Mother Angelica, you need prayer.' I was thinking, why don't you just buzz off, I'm doing fine, thank you. But I listened. 'You need the baptism of the Holy Spirit.' I told him I received the Holy Spirit when I was baptized. I really just wanted him to get lost."

Reluctantly, the priest left, but he returned on several occasions and persisted, saying he simply wanted to pray over Mother as she sat in a chair.

"Well, is that all you want?" she asked, finally caving in to his request. "If I'd have known that, I could have gotten rid of you a long time ago!" she joked. Muttering under her breath, Mother walked with the priest to the building and proceeded to sit down in a chair. The priest laid his hands on her head and began to pray that the Holy Spirit would come upon her in a new and powerful way. It seemed rather uneventful, and when he had finished his prayer, Mother looked up and asked, "Is that it?"

"That's it," he replied confidently with a crafty smile on his face. He acted as if he knew something that Mother didn't, which as events would bear out, indeed proved to be the case.

Minutes later, the priest disappeared in his car, leaving Mother and the Sisters wondering exactly what all the commotion was about.

A week passed and the Sisters continued to work on their ambitious landscape design, which was built around the statue of Our Lady of the Angels. Mother was fairly secure in the knowledge that nothing untoward had transpired as a result of the aggressive priest's unusual prayer. Then, suddenly, Mother Angelica was hit by a terrible cold. She went to bed feeling exhausted and miserable. The Sisters waited on her, checking in every few hours.

"There I sat, propped up in my bed, with my Bible in front of me. For some reason, I had decided to read the Gospel of St. John aloud, 'In the beginning was the Word and the Word was with God and the Word was God . . .' I was suddenly overpowered in the Spirit—it was a totally new experience for me," Mother Angelica whispers in a hushed tone, still awestruck by the event.

At that moment, Sister Regina, a now nun in the community, appeared in Mother Angelica's room with a glass of orange juice. Sensing something unusual, Sister Regina stopped short of Mother's bed, placing the glass on a nightstand nearby. The Sister began to speak but Mother Angelica did not respond verbally, instead making urgent hand motions indicating she could not talk. The younger nun quickly retreated from the room, puzzled by the sudden loss of voice. Surprised by something she did not fully understand and could not explain, Mother Angelica lay motionless in her bed for what seemed like hours.

Then, slowly, she got up and walked from her room, only later noticing that all of her previously severe cold symptoms had completely vanished. She had been totally overcome by a sense of God's presence in her room and in her being. It was a sensation beyond description that seemed to parallel the stories of the early Franciscan monks who had likewise been "slain in the Spirit"—overpowered by God in a kind of holy paralysis. She felt a heightened sense of reality—a scintillating excitement tempered by a magnified reverence for Christ she had rarely felt to such an intense degree.

The sensation seemed to well up from within her innermost being. She felt a new sense of purpose, although she had few specifics at that moment. It was if God were somehow saying, "I am preparing you for something special and unique." She felt awesome power. She was renewed. She would be ready for God's direction.

How, she wondered later, could she ever tell the others what had happened? Walking alone outdoors to the edge of the property, she paced back and forth, contemplating the circumstances leading up to this unanticipated moment of divine intervention. She pondered these things, remaining silent about them for more than two months.

As winter closed in upon the little Irondale community, Mother Angelica shared, ever so carefully at first, that something had happened to her—something special that she wanted to pass on. The Sisters apparently had ears to hear because they eagerly responded to Mother's promptings.

As the Easter season approached, she became increasingly more specific in her prayers and more obvious in her intent— she wished that all the Sisters could experience the empowering she had felt six months earlier. Taking the Sisters aside one by one, she prayed over them and, one by one, the Sisters came into a new dimension of relationship with God through the Holy Spirit. There was a new vitality in the air at Our Lady of the Angels Monastery. The renewal, about which all the Sisters had been hearing, had suddenly become much more than hearsay—it had become a reality in their own midst. Already a tightly knit religious "family," the experience drew them even closer together.

"Over the years people have asked if we are Pentecostals, or if we are a charismatic monastery. They wanted to know if we speak in tongues, prophesy and experience all kinds of miracles. I'm not totally comfortable labeling this renewal process in such ways," Mother Angelica says today. "Of course, these are all legitimate gifts of the Spirit—we find them in the Bible and we read about them in the history of the church, going all the way back to the time of the apostles. But this is not our identity in the community. Each individual Sister is charismatic in her own special way—each Sister is, as I like to say, Spirit enhanced. Each one therefore makes her own very unique contribution to the community as a result of her own renewal experience. But people are enamored with the gifts of the Spirit and with the miraculous. Yes, we utilize these gifts, but we do it in a monastic way. It has enriched our prayer lives, our liturgy and our call to perpetual adoration. We have been enriched but not changed in our vocations."

Obviously, this chapter in the lives of the Sisters of Our Lady of the Angels Monastery was—and remains—a special blessing. The fruits became clearly evident and the benefits readily discernible. Upon deeper reflection and more widespread observation, however, Mother Angelica began to see some hidden dangers.

"I began to see that people were leaving the church and the sacraments," Mother Angelica explains. "They were responding to the powerful emotionalism and, at times, sensationalism found in this movement and they were not prepared to handle it. They weren't really fully grounded in their faith. They became spiritual drifters, seeking an experience instead of Christ."

Feeling a sense of urgency, Mother began speaking and teaching on her own renewal process, balancing it against the critical need to adhere to the sacramental life and to remain rooted in the sound doctrine of the faith. She found herself going after the lost sheep—and finding some. Her scripture class for lay people was based on this need and lasted more than four years.

"I found that people needed to be taught the basics to pro-

vide them with an unshakeable foundation for their faith,"
she says. "There was, and I think there still is, a tremendous
need for instruction and teaching to go along with the power
and excitement of the charismatic renewal."

Mother Angelica was becoming well known throughout the
Birmingham area. She was constantly being asked to lead
prayer meetings and Bible studies that crossed denominational
lines. It came as no surprise when she was invited to participate in a committee meeting of the diocese that focused on
helping to meet the needs of people to grow spiritually. Prayer,
she was convinced, would make the difference. People needed
to learn how to pray and how to grow spiritually through the
commitment to prayer. As the date for the diocesan committee
meeting approached, she pulled the Sisters together to collab-
orate on a small booklet on prayer.

"We were all so excited as we helped Mother find scripture
passages for the booklet which she called *Journey into Prayer,*"
Sister Raphael says. "She wanted to show our heavenly Father's love and tenderness for us and how we could learn to
pray more effectively. She would then submit her booklet to
the committee and in doing so help to strengthen the spiritual
lives of Catholic lay people. We made folders and copied the
materials so each member of the committee could review the
content for discussion."

Journey into Prayer became a booklet heavily laced with relevant scriptures from both New and Old Testaments, structured to meet various needs including meditations for private
prayer, family prayer, retreats, spiritual growth and prayer
communities.

The booklet explored the three levels of prayer found in the
Bible verse that exhorts, "Ask and you shall receive; seek and
you shall find; knock and it shall be opened" (Matt. 7:7).
Verses, songs, reflections and teaching fill the twenty-nine–
page pamphlet, making it a formidable tool for any inquiring
soul. It was Mother Angelica's desire to "help the praying

community attain a closer relationship with God and neighbor—a relationship fed by the sacraments and sustained through prayer,'' as she stated in the booklet's introduction.

Mother took the material to the committee meeting, confident she had forged a response to the needs of parishioners throughout the diocese. This, she thought to herself, could even become a ministry of the monastery—a special ministry of communication in sharing the Sisters' own prayer vocation in a meaningful way to the outside world. Certainly it fit the spirit and letter of the Second Vatican Council's call to renewal and evangelization. Perhaps it was for this purpose that the Holy Spirit had empowered and emboldened the Sisters to produce a work aimed at teaching and inspiring the faithful and, with God's blessing, propel the renewal with responsible instruction.

Mother arrived at the committee meeting early with an armful of material that she passed out for review and for commentary. As the meeting drew on into the afternoon, various plans emerged for meeting the critical needs of the laity, which included parish and home visitation and, to Mother's agitation, more committee meetings.

"What about this booklet?" she finally asked, a bit impatient with the bureaucratic committee. There was a strained silence and committee members looked at one another, shrugging.

"Well, we have decided to go with a plan to have special committees carry out a program of meetings and parish visits," one member responded. "Maybe we could use your material as a possible third phase of the operation."

Mother was stunned. She returned to the monastery crushed and dejected. Her promising booklet project had been summarily relegated to last place on the committee's priority list, yet she remained convinced that such a publishing project could benefit those who really needed instruction and encouragement.

"All of our efforts, it seemed, had been for nothing. But the rest of us were all committed to the idea of continuing to publish Mother's ideas in booklet form," Sister Raphael remembers. "We encouraged her to move ahead. We knew what she had to offer because she would first run her ideas by us in our daily lesson time."

Uplifted by the Sisters, Mother Angelica picked herself up, dusted herself off and said, "Well, let's get on with it! We've got work to do and we'll just do it on our own."

It was a new beginning—an entirely different phase of ministry for the Sisters. They obtained copyrights, secured the bishop's *imprimatur* and hired out the actual printing. Soon, the five and one-half by eight and one-half–inch books were coming off the press by the thousands and distributed free of charge.

Mother had a seemingly endless supply of topics for her booklets. She was regularly tapping her creative wellsprings in order to keep up with a hefty schedule of speaking engagements and teaching sessions. Among these commitments was an interdenominational women's scripture study group that met weekly and, of course, Mother Angelica was always ready with a provocative topic for discussion. Eventually, more than 250 talks were given by Mother and recorded on audio cassettes. Much of the material, the Sisters felt, should be written and published in book form. Wasting no time, they set out to create more booklets.

"As each booklet formed in Mother's mind, she would begin writing on a yellow legal pad. Once her idea was down in writing, she would bring the Sisters a lesson from it and, of course, we would respond to the idea," says Sister Raphael.

The booklets stirred up a fair amount of interest as they emerged from the monastery. A faithful readership developed, people who eagerly anticipated Mother's next release. The local news media even began tracking Mother's new publishing project and, on occasion, would dispatch reporters to interview the "publishing nun."

"Tell me, Mother Angelica," one reporter queried, "just where does your material come from?"

"Well, you know, the sentences just seem to form—it's like I see them in my mind first, then I just write them down. When the light turns out in my head, I know the book is finished," she answered.

"I see," came the incredulous reply.

"And Mother's manuscripts are never edited once she writes them. We just type it up, proof it for spelling and take it to the printer!" Sister Raphael added, explaining that she was also the design artist for the layout and the book covers.

"You're a better writer than I am, Mother," the reporter responded, jotting notes as he spoke. "I get edited regularly— but then, you undoubtedly have a better pipeline to your boss than I do to mine!"

With each new article, the Sisters of Our Lady of the Angels Monastery became more widely known. They were no longer simply Southern nun curiosities. The family of those benefiting from their new ministry, as well as supporters of their work, continued to grow rapidly, especially after the format of the booklets changed, making them more cost efficient and easily distributed.

"We began designing and printing smaller, condensed versions of Mother's original writings," Sister Raphael explains. "By using just one sheet of paper, we created a twelve-page booklet which was much easier to pass out and cheaper to produce. We began calling them mini-books. We gave them away to tourists, business people downtown and placed them in gas stations, restaurants, hospitals—even restrooms. By the thousands, we prayed over them and sowed them like seed throughout the country."

Within months, requests for the mini-books were arriving from all over the world. Everyone who asked received them without charge although many willingly donated to the project, which helped sustain production. The results were worth the involvement in this increasingly costly undertaking.

Cards, letters and phone calls began to flow into the monastery. People even drove across the country to meet the Sisters. Often, mail arrived telling tales of spiritual renewal and emotional healing. On numerous occasions letters arrived that revealed the life-and-death realities of hopeless individuals who had come upon Mother's writings:

> Dear Mother Angelica:
>
> I hope this letter actually reaches you. I feel I owe my life to you. Last year, after my husband left me and I lost my job in a large insurance company, I became very depressed. I have no living family so I felt truly hopeless. I decided to take my own life. I had nothing left to live for. I stopped at a phone booth to call a friend but there was no answer and I became even more depressed. Then I looked down and found your mini-book. I don't know why but I read it and cried. I was raised a Catholic but left the church years ago. After reading your booklet, I prayed and decided to go to a priest. That was six months ago. My life has changed. My problems aren't all gone but I have you to thank for giving me hope. God bless you!
>
> S.K.

Others began to write with equally moving stories, telling of answered prayer, renewed faith and restored hope. The Sisters were overjoyed and thankful to see how the mini-books had reaped a substantial harvest in the lives of people throughout the country.

"We're onto something!" Mother proclaimed to the Sisters one day. "But we've got a major problem. Our printer says she can no longer print our mini-books and we all know we can't afford commercial printing rates." Mother had written and supervised the publication of seventeen mini-books by this time and was not about to halt production because of something as trivial as printing complications.

"What will we do, Mother?" one Sister asked.

"We can't stop publishing now," another spoke up.

"We'll just get our own press and print our own books!" Mother proclaimed after a few long, silent moments. The Sisters laughed. Then the laughter stopped. They had seen that expression before.

"I'm serious."

There would be no stopping Mother Angelica.

CHAPTER SEVEN

---※---

The Eternal Word

"Faith is having one foot on the ground and the other up in the air waiting for the Lord to put the ground under it," Mother Angelica maintains, ever mindful that faith must be a key component of any pioneering ministry. Judging by the response of a few "Job's comforters" who observed her decision to go to a major in-house printing operation, she had placed her foot squarely on a banana peel. People could not envision cloistered nuns laboring in a print shop with ink on their hands, and everyone knows how complex and temperamental printing equipment can be.

"You can't just go out and be a print shop overnight," one seasoned veteran of the offset trade said to the nuns. "Even if you do manage to purchase and install the machinery, who's gonna fix it when it breaks down?"

But Mother wouldn't be dissuaded. By 1976 she had written 50 mini-books and recorded 150 audio-cassette teaching tapes. She knew she had something significant to say and she also knew a good printing press would let her say it to hundreds of thousands of people. She could not forget that powerful verse from the Gospel of St. John that she read as she lay sick in bed: "In the beginning was the Word . . . ." The Spirit of God had seared the scripture passage into her heart like a brand with the command to, quite literally, spread the Word.

The next step had to be a printing press—there was just no way around it.

"I'll be honest with you," Mother Angelica says, "we didn't know the difference between a pound of ink and a ream of paper, but we were determined to go through with this thing. Sure, there's always the chance of failure—but look at Peter. He always had his foot in his mouth and he made all kinds of mistakes and promises he couldn't live up to. But every time he failed he tried again. We had to do the same thing. Working on a sure thing is not working on faith."

"We knew there was tremendous value in those booklets," Sister Raphael attests. "More and more letters came in every day from people whose lives had been changed, and that's what the mini-books were all about—touching people's lives. It has always been Mother's intention to reach people in the church pews. They need to know how to live Christianity on a daily basis and how to be holy. In Mother's experience, many people will attend church on Sunday and then simply put Jesus in a box during the rest of the week. It is the lives of these people Mother was attempting to touch in a meaningful way, and the tremendous response demonstrated to all of us that we were on the right track."

When the time seemed right, Mother took Sister Regina with her to a commercial printing-press showroom, determined that she would walk away with some kind of a deal on a printing press. As she walked through the showroom floor, she examined the presses, running her hands over the gleaming new equipment. Pretty complicated looking, she thought, but nothing the Sisters can't handle. Within minutes a salesman glided casually toward the nuns, a pleasant smile on his face. "And how many I help you, Sisters?" he asked.

"We need a press," Mother responded.

"What kind of printing do you do?"

"We need to print these." Mother handed him one of her

booklets, explaining the story of how her mini-book ministry began and her plans for future printing projects.

"What kind of equipment are you using now?" the salesman asked.

"We don't have any printing equipment and we have never used any printing equipment—that's why I'm here." Mother was growing impatient. Why was he asking all these questions? All she wanted was a printing press. "We want to print these," she said waving the book in the air for emphasis. "Give me the manager."

Mother repeated her story to the manager. It was apparent to her that he was also not ready to take her seriously—and she was not about to waste time "beating around the bush." She became exasperated with technical questions and a seeming lack of genuine interest.

"Look," she asked flatly, "do you want to sell me a press or not?"

"Yes, of course, but these are quite complicated pieces of equipment—how will you learn to use it?" he asked.

"If it takes more than twenty minutes to learn, forget it," she said, walking toward a press that caught her eye. "How about this one—this one looks fine to me. It has a couple of buttons and a couple of gadgets—I'm sure we could learn to use this thing."

"That model sells for $9,000," the salesman replied.

"I'll take it," Mother said, swallowing hard with the knowledge that she had a mere $200 in her possession. Sister Regina, perched on a stool nearby, nearly fell off in shock but maintained a deceptively calm facade.

"And, of course, you know you'll need a cutter and a stapler to go along with the press," the man quickly followed up.

"Oh, yes," Mother whispered, tightening up inside over the increasing financial commitment she was making. Sister Regina slumped further and further under the weight of it all.

"Mother!" the younger nun exclaimed incredulously as

they left the building, "Do you know what you've done? Where will we get the money?"

"The bank. They've got lots of money and we need some!" Mother Angelica responded cheerfully.

Mother went from bank to bank in unsuccessful attempts to secure a loan. Her resolve had begun to fade just a bit as she decided to take one final shot at funding her printing press. Again, she heard the disappointing news that the institution could extend no loan.

"Why won't you give us a loan?" she demanded of the banker across the table from her. They had all begun to look— and sound—alike. She could feel her anger beginning to rise.

"You have no collateral for a loan," came the crisp reply.

"I have a monastery that's paid for," Mother countered.

"Mother Angelica," he answered, "what if you were to default on the loan? Can you imagine how we would be viewed? This city would kill us if we began foreclosure proceedings against the monastery. Tell me, what other assets do you have?"

"If I had any, I certainly wouldn't be here right now, would I?" Mother shot back.

"Okay, what is your monthly income? Tell me something about the monastery cash flow."

"I don't know—it's not the end of the month, so I can't tell you."

The loan officer lowered his voice to a whisper and continued. "Are you asking me to give you a loan on faith? Do you really expect me to face the board of directors of this institution and tell them that I gave Mother Angelica a $13,000 loan on faith?"

"Yes."

"I can't do that!"

"Pagan!" she exclaimed.

She left the bank in a state of utter disappointment, her patience exhausted. Why must everything be so complicated, she wondered. Even more disturbing, why was she not taken seriously in the business community? Perhaps it was the fact that she was a woman—and a nun at that! She would simply have to try harder. She was determined to follow through with what she believed to be God's will for her community.

It was very apparent that a pattern had emerged in Mother Angelica's life. It was a pattern of commitment to God, discerning His will, pursuing that will with a vengeance and confronting the obstacle that would most certainly present itself somewhere along the path. But beyond the obstacle was always God's provision which oftentimes came in unexplainable ways. Mother Angelica had been refused by every bank she visited. Of course she was extremely disappointed, but she began to look up—she knew that God would come through as He always did.

As the delivery date for the printing equipment drew near, a long-time friend stopped by the monastery to visit Mother and the Sisters. "Hey," Mother asked in jest, "how would you like to lend me $10,000!"

"Sure!" he answered without missing a beat. Mother was momentarily speechless.

"You are joking, aren't you?" she laughed nervously.

"No, are you?" he asked.

"I was joking to begin with, but I'm dead serious now!" Mother replied with high enthusiasm. That afternoon she had a signed check in her hand for $10,000. The Sisters rejoiced, having managed the other $3,000 through their own fund-raising efforts.

"See? We do all we can, and God does the rest!" Mother exclaimed. When asked if she could repay the loan in ninety days, Mother said simply, "No. But God can."

The exhilaration of this timely provision was short-lived. Mother immediately announced that she intended to bring all printing into the monastery. That meant acquiring the hardware needed to create camera-ready art, negatives and plates. The special camera equipment alone would cost $4,500.

"Over our protests, she went ahead and ordered everything," Sister Raphael explains. "It wasn't so much the cost we objected to but the fact that we knew it took training to use all that technical gear—none of us felt at all qualified. Since Mother had me in mind to operate the camera, she ordered the one that was most simple to use," she laughs.

When the camera equipment arrived, serious complications cropped up. The enormous sink used in the developing process would not fit through the monastery door. The only solution would seem to have been the dismantling of the doorway and the destruction of part of a wall.

An irritated delivery workman confronted Mother Angelica. "Didn't anyone around here bother to measure the door for the delivery of this sink?" he demanded.

"Have you actually tried to get it through the doorway?" Mother asked.

"You must be kidding me—this sink will not fit through that door!" he shouted, gesturing wildly with his gloved hands.

Mother and the Sisters examined the sink closely, then scrutinized the dimensions of the monastery door. It seemed obvious to all that there was no way the sink could be delivered.

"Well, let's pray over it," Mother insisted after another disheartening examination.

"God almighty couldn't get this sink through that door," the workman exclaimed. "It took three of us to load this thing on our truck and now you're telling me you want us to unload it just to prove you wrong!" Beyond patience, he shook his head.

"You try it. I'll pray." Mother Angelica was eyeball to eyeball with the burly truck driver.

In minutes the three men were groaning as they offloaded the unwieldy, heavy metal sink, muttering under their breath. Mother and the Sisters huddled around quietly praying. To everyone's astonishment, the sink slid through the doorway with inches to spare. The workmen walked back and forth, unbelieving, reexamining the doorway closely. There was a stony silence.

"I just don't believe it," one man said flatly. "It's not possible." The men walked sheepishly away while Mother and the Sisters beamed.

"It was a true miracle—we just never knew whether the Lord shrunk the sink or widened the door!" exclaims Sister Raphael, who had observed the episode with high interest. "But that's not the end of it," she continued. "In the midst of all these developments, we received a visit from dear friends from out of town. Of course, this couple wanted to know all that was happening with us and the monastery. After showing them around, we told them the story of the sink and showed them our plans for setting up a print shop. Just before the couple left, they decided to celebrate the wife's birthday by covering the cost of the camera equipment. They wrote out a check on the spot!"

Still, the wonders didn't cease. The Sisters purchased a cutting machine and had it operating for weeks, cutting extremely small versions of Mother's mini-books before they were told by the salesman that the size they wanted would be impossible for the equipment to handle.

"But we're already doing it!" the Sisters protested.

"That's impossible," came the expert reply. "This I have got to see!"

Of course, Mother Angelica had prayed over the equipment and invited the salesman to a demonstration of its capabilities. Picking up a stack of mini-books, she confidently loaded them into the cutting machine and snapped on the switch. Immediately, in a loud rush, the books began shooting out in pairs like rounds from a machine gun, neatly trimmed to size.

"Wait minute—how did you do that?" the dealer asked in amazement.

"I don't know, let's sneak up on it!" Mother laughed, leaning over the machine.

"The man called the manufacturing plant in Michigan, telling them of our equipment that was slitting a book to a three by six–inch size. They told him that it simply couldn't be done. 'Don't tell me what they can't do,' he yelled back at them, 'I'm telling you what they're doing!' " Sister Raphael says.

"We have a miracle a day!" Mother Angelica told an interviewer from the *Our Sunday Visitor* newspaper, which reported on the monastery's rapidly growing book ministry. Even the most skeptical observers went away scratching their heads for an explanation of events transpiring among the Franciscan Sisters in Irondale. The stories of Mother's exploits were beginning to make the rounds across the country. There was increasing demand for the mini-books and for interviews with Mother Angelica.

As the Sisters considered their print-shop needs, they decided to purchase the kind of equipment that could do the greatest amount of work in the shortest amount of time. Among their overriding considerations was their unyielding commitment to the cloister—to contemplative prayer and perpetual adoration before the Blessed Sacrament. Their Franciscan rule for prayer and work were to be adhered to strictly. The Sisters would not be deterred from this priority. To them, the printing of mini-books for distribution to the public was simply the fruit of their spiritual union with God in prayer.

Soon the self-taught Sisters were operating their printing press like experts. The great demand for free books led to the purchase of three more presses. Sister Emmanuel emerged as a champion press-person, causing even professional printers to stare in amazement as she simultaneously kept four presses running in the monastery print shop. With sleeves rolled up, and an ink-spattered apron tied around her slight frame, Sister Emmanuel, with the help of the other Sisters, managed to crank out 25,000 books a day, producing 6 million the following year. By 1978 the Sisters were operating presses worth more than $120,000, printing booklets of all sizes.

"As our operation expanded, more equipment was required. We had two large binding and stapling machines and a heavy-duty folder, plus all of our typesetting equipment. We simply needed more room; so we began building an addition to the monastery to accommodate our growing publishing apostolate," Sister Raphael explains. "With only $200 in our bank account, we started this building project. Each week enough contributions for the booklets came in to cover the building project. And when the new print room was all finished we placed a sign over the door that read: 'WE DON'T KNOW WHAT WE'RE DOING, BUT WE'RE GETTING GOOD AT IT!' "

Favorable reports continued to filter back to Mother and the Sisters, encouraging them to expand their work. Key lay people from all walks of life demonstrated increasing interest in the monastery's work and began to gravitate toward Mother and the Sisters, volunteering their services.

"It's amazing how Mother Angelica's booklets have affected people's lives," one layman reports. "One man wrote in that he was on his way to kill himself when he found one of Mother's booklets on a park bench. He read it and was so moved by the goodness of God that he decided to live. I can think of another case where a prostitute read one of the booklets and was motivated to change her life. But it's not simply the books," he observes. "It's the Lord working in the lives of His people through these books which were all written in a prayerful spirit, while Mother Angelica prayed before the Blessed Sacrament."

The Sisters upped their production—they printed hundreds of thousands of booklets a month, on presses they were never trained to operate and never had the money to buy. They continued to manage all of this while working four and one-half hours a day, six days a week, careful to spend their five hours in prayer each day.

"There are three things the Sisters have proven through all of this," Mother Angelica says. "First of all, God always seems to take care of the bills when we are really trying to do His work—it has never failed us yet. Secondly, we can do His work, as busy as we might be, and still have time to pray. Finally, if we are not spending time in prayer as we should, we cannot do His work."

By this time, Mother's booklets were being distributed in all fifty states and in thirty-seven foreign countries in various translations including French, Spanish and Vietnamese. In many places, the booklets were being used in conjunction with catechetical studies and evangelization programs. Volunteer workers, including grade-school children, eagerly distributed the materials in large quantities.

Through a series of teachings at Our Lady of the Angels Monastery and training programs, Mother instructed enthusiastic Catholic lay people in presenting her teaching and her booklets in a nationwide outreach program that she called Catholic Family Missionary Alliance (CFMA). Her goal was to provide every interested parish in the United States with a five-step program in renewal and family spirituality. Mother designed the program to be relevant to single people, married couples, families, priests and religious.

Beginning with a handful of interested participants, CFMA grew to encompass more than 8,000 men and women, including a core group of "guardians" who maintained special roles in the organization. At the same time, Birmingham Bishop Joseph Vath granted Mother Angelica permission to leave the cloister to personally share her message of spirituality across the country.

"We were particularly encouraged and motivated by Pope Paul VI's encyclical on evangelism," remembers Sister Raphael. "The pope stated that *now* was the time to evangelize and that it was the duty of every man, woman and child of the church. We continued to print, package and ship mini-books around the country. At one eucharistic congress, a zealous group of six children passed out more than 150,000 mini-books and leaflets!''

As operations expanded at the monastery, more room was required for the growing inventory of equipment. Yet another addition was constructed—"the miracle room"—boosting the printing ministry to new levels.

Mother Angelica's daily lessons with the Sisters continued to reflect the growth of their already far-reaching ministry and her underlying philosophy. Criticized for taking what appeared to be wild risks and doubted by those who did not believe she could pull off the improbable, Mother Angelica addressed the Sisters one morning, sharing her thoughts with them.

"You know, so often we toss our good ideas to mental committees in our own heads. We literally talk ourselves right out of doing what God really wants. The process of doing God's will," she stated, "is really quite simple. First, we determine the purpose of the action we believe has been directed by God. It is always to promote the church and further His kingdom. An inspiration suggests a way in which to achieve this. Then, I jump right in! I begin the process immediately. If the Lord keeps evolving the plan, I push on and look for the fruit, taking the risk of failure. I would rather fail by trying than fail totally by not trying at all."

Mother looked at her willing team and restated a phrase that had become her motto—one the Sisters had come to live by: "Unless we are willing to do the ridiculous, God will not do the miraculous."

Indeed, thus far in Mother Angelica's life as a Franciscan nun, she had been accused of doing the ridiculous which, as she aptly pointed out, served to unleash the great power of God in accomplishing His will. As Mother continues to point out, however, God's intervention does not alleviate her and the Sisters of the anxieties and frustrations associated with such an enormous undertaking.

"I've got to tell you," she states firmly, "I have been a complainer, I have been rebellious and grumpy, I have experienced great frustration and I have even been mad at God and the church at times. I have looked up and said 'Why me, Lord?' And do you know what His response is? It is as if He has turned back to me and said, 'Yes, Angelica, and why *me?*' Now, that really puts me in my place with the knowledge that my pain and problems are nothing compared to what Jesus endured on our behalf."

It is this realization that has inspired Mother Angelica and the Sisters to greater works and sacrifices. It has been this understanding that has fortified them for the challenges that were yet to come—challenges that would one day dwarf the giants they had been battling up to now.

Mother Angelica's printing and book apostolate multiplied her ability to share the gospel far beyond her wildest dreams. She was not prepared, however, for the incredible demand for more written material and for personal appearances. People across the country who had been exposed to her writings now wanted to meet the personality behind those teachings. Mother was able to amplify her propagation of the gospel through the willing volunteers who had eagerly gathered around her and by occasionally venturing out of the cloister to address groups of people on special occasions. Even with the bishop's permission to go out six times a year, Mother Angelica and the Sisters began to realize that they were only scratching the surface in reaching out to those in spiritual need.

Mother Angelica began carefully choosing her speaking engagements in order to involve the media as much as possible.

When invitations arose for television interviews, she accepted them with the understanding that TV had become a powerful force in reaching many times more people than could possibly hear her in person.

A number of Christian television stations, fascinated with this charismatic Franciscan nun from the South, began extending invitations to her for interviews. One of the first was Channel 38 in Chicago, a UHF television station owned and operated by evangelical Protestants. Mother flew to Chicago with Sister Joseph, ever mindful of the scriptural injunction to go out two by two.

"That was a real turning point for us," Mother Angelica remembers. "Here was this tiny television station on top of a large, downtown building. I looked around, saw the cameras and video equipment and a few people operating out of a tiny studio. I marveled at how many people were being reached by this ministry. As I walked into the studio I said, 'Lord, I gotta have one of these!' Of course, I did ask myself the question, what on earth would twelve cloistered nuns do with a television studio? But I quickly put these negative thoughts aside knowing that's the quickest way on earth to stifle the Spirit."

In March of 1978, Mother Angelica's vision for communicating the gospel had just taken another quantum leap. As she and Sister Joseph drove away from the studio, Mother Angelica repeated herself, her excitement increasing by the second.

"I really gotta have one of those!" Mother rubbed her hands together as she spoke.

Sister Joseph simply prayed, knowing full well that when Mother decided she wanted something, she usually got it. As she sought the Lord in prayer, she was specifically impressed that Mother was right. God seemed to confirm that the air waves indeed belonged to Him and that He would entrust Mother with a media ministry. She shared her thoughts and impressions with Mother that very moment.

"Are you joking?" Mother asked Sister Joseph.

"I don't think He was!" Sister Joseph replied.

By the time the two nuns returned to the monastery, she knew exactly what she wanted to do although she had no idea how to go about it.

"You know, this is the really exciting part of any new ministry," Mother Angelica says. "Just plunging in out of obedience without the full knowledge of where to begin—it's wonderful! I am fully convinced that we have come to rely too heavily on corporate methods to get things done. We have to have everything planned out, all the money up front, all the talent lined up and all the capabilities nailed down in some kind of absolute guarantee of success before we ever begin. By that time, we forget what we started out to do in the first place! Now, where is the faith in that approach?"

Wasting no time, Mother Angelica immediately began inquiring through her own network of friends and acquaintances about possibilities for television production. Jean Morris, an Episcopalian lay person, long committed to Mother's work, located a small video operation in the Birmingham area. Together they conceived the idea for a limited video-tape series, entitled "Our Hermitage." From the beginning, production proved much tougher than Mother had anticipated. There was so much involved—cameras, lights, temperamental microphones, set designs, split-second timing and many unforeseen "glitches" that could arise any moment in the midst of taping sessions.

"I don't know how many times I heard the director say 'Cut!' " Mother remembers. "It was awful. I walked on the set like a baby elephant, dragging the mike cord behind me. I sat down looking like Grandma Moses with a Mickey Mouse voice—it seemed like a real disaster."

"As we rode home that afternoon," Sister Raphael recalls, "Mother was a bit discouraged. She said 'Why don't we just admit that I don't have it and quit?' But Jean and I were totally committed to the idea and told her emphatically that she had to go through with it. We knew she could do it.''

After a number of aborted attempts, a new set design and several sessions in the studio, Mother Angelica walked away with a program on tape that had cost $1,000 to produce. Mother was convinced it would be a perfect program to air on the Christian Broadcasting Network. She dispatched Jean to hand-carry their pilot program for review by CBN producers. Within two weeks Mother Angelica received a phone call from the Christian Broadcasting Network offices. They had been praying, they said, for some kind of Catholic program at the very time Mother Angelica sent the tape.

Mother was overjoyed that CBN wanted to use the program and overwhelmed to hear that they wanted her to make sixty more! In her enthusiasm, she immediately agreed to do sixty more tapes without realizing this could mean in excess of $60,000 for production expenses. The scramble was on. Jean Morris, Sister Raphael and Mother Angelica, mindful that they had a golden opportunity to air a television program on the well-known CBN network, leapt into action.

Within days, a local television station had been located that would accommodate their video-production plans. Sister Raphael and Jean quickly designed a set and supervised its construction, creating the visual impression of a cozy living room complete with fireplace and flower arrangements.

The first day of taping finally arrived. Mother, Sister Raphael and Jean Morris scurried about nervously in preparation for producing the very first program of their sixty-program series. As the crew erected the set in the studio, Jean applied the finishing touches of makeup to Mother Angelica. Sister Raphael hovered in the control booth, planning camera shots and preparing the opening sequence which was shot earlier. With lights and cameras adjusted and in place, Mother Angelica whispered a brief prayer as she listened to the floor director count the seconds down.

"Five, four, three . . ." She felt butterflies in her stomach but betrayed not a bit of nervousness. "Two, one, roll tape!"

Mother leaned into the camera with a kindly yet piercing stare. She spoke as if to one needy soul, sharing a homily of hope and love.

"Here's the really amazing thing about the way Mother handled television," says Sister Raphael. "With no notes or cue cards, Mother simply began to speak out of her heart. It was much the same as when she wrote her mini-books. She would simply rely on the Holy Spirit to give her the words, which would come to her only when the tape began to roll. Mother would speak for exactly twenty-eight minutes, the length of a half-hour tape. After that, she took a five-minute break, then sat down to tape another program. Every afternoon, we would return to the monastery with four programs on two-inch video-tape masters. We also had a number of video-tape cassettes of our programs. Mother would always begin her taping sessions with a few words of prayer with the crew and, invariably, they would come up to her at the end of a taping session and ask her all kinds of questions—they really came to appreciate her sincerity and ability."

In an extremely short period of time, sixty programs in the "Our Hermitage" series were "in the can" and ready for airing. This series taught the basics from the gospels and aired throughout the country via the CBN Network. Virtually overnight, Mother Angelica became a familiar face to millions of viewers throughout the country.

Encouraged by their first real video success, Mother Angelica planned a subsequent series entitled, "In His Sandals," commentaries on the epistles. Once again, Jean Morris and Sister Raphael were key figures in supporting Mother Angelica through the second run of tapings. A more elaborate set was designed, Sister Raphael became increasingly more familiar with the technical end of production and, overall, Mother Angelica became much more comfortable and proficient at communicating her message through the eye of the camera.

Things seemed to go better with each program until the seventeenth segment of "In His Sandals" was produced. It was at this time that Mother Angelica and the Sisters learned that the television station they had hired to produce their programs was scheduled to telecast a controversial film entitled *The Word*, which many believed to be sacrilegious. The plot in the upcoming feature revolved around the discovery of an ancient scroll that "proved" that Jesus was not God, did not die on the cross and was not resurrected.

Mother was furious. Confronting the station manager, she minced no words in condemning the film, describing the damage she believed would be done to the viewing public through its influence.

"I know you believe yourself to be a Christian," Mother Angelica said to the station manager.

"Yes, of course," came his reply.

"Then how can you allow this blasphemous material to be telecast over your television station?" she asked impatiently.

"Do you really think God cares what we do down here?" he asked.

"Yes, of course, He cares," Mother affirmed, "and I care."

"Are you telling me what kind of programs I should run on my own station?" he demanded.

"I've been coming here for three months and I have never said a word to you about your crummy programs! But I'll tell you now I think you do have crummy programs on your station." Mother was under control—but just barely. She was reaching the boiling point. She waited for his reply.

"Well, I intend to show the movie," he answered defiantly.

"If that's your final decision," she replied, "then I intend to make mine. I will not sign your contract to air my programs on your station and, furthermore, I refuse to produce any more programs in your studio. It is against my principles to condone blasphemy!'' Mother was steaming, determined she would not contribute in any way to what she considered to be a blatant violation of her conscience.

"You can't do that!'' he hissed. "You leave here and you're off television permanently. There's no other studio within a hundred miles of here—you have no choice. You need us.''

"That's where you're wrong,'' she countered. "I don't need you. I need only God. I'll buy my own cameras and I will build my own studio and, as sure as I'm standing here, I will tape my own programs.''

"You can't do that—there's no way,'' he stated confidently.

"You just watch me,'' Mother Angelica replied with boundless determination.

Upon her return to the monastery, Mother shared with all the Sisters the disturbing events of the day. They were behind her 100 percent. "But I blew it,'' Mother admitted, telling them how she cancelled her production schedule with the studio. "I even told him I'd build my own studio and create my own programs, but quite honestly, I wouldn't know where to begin.''

Mother slumped in her chair, certain she had made a terrific mistake. Where would she turn? The Sisters had an idea. They gathered around her and assured her that she could do it. "I know!'' one Sister exclaimed gleefully. "We can turn our garage into a studio!'' The other Sisters cheered in unanimous agreement.

Spontaneously, they all walked briskly down the stairs behind the monastery, examining the 1,500 concrete blocks remaining after completion of the printing-shop addition. They were about to build a garage for their community car and an old tractor. Mother eyed the excavation which had already begun and summoned one of the workmen, issuing instructions for a longer and wider foundation.

Yes, she thought to herself. This will be our own television studio! We're going through with it. God will provide.

This was the beginning of what would become the Eternal Word Television Network. There it was—bare earth, only partially excavated and prepared for what was to have been a garage. No nails had been driven; not one block rested upon another, yet Mother's mind was filled with images of studio space, cameras, lights, video-tape equipment and a crew. Where would it all come from? She had nowhere else to turn but to God Himself. Firmly believing He had presented a mandate to communicate His love to a waiting world, she cast herself at His feet in prayer, along with the other Sisters.

I must be on the right track, she grinned to herself. I've really done the ridiculous! Now, it's up to God. He'll have to do the miraculous.

CHAPTER EIGHT

✳

What's in a Name?

"In the beginning was the Word and the Word was with God and the Word was God . . ." Mother Angelica's thoughts would frequently return to the words in St. John's Gospel. She would never forget those empowering moments of visitation from the Holy Spirit as she read that passage from her Bible as she lay sick in bed nearly eight years before.

The Word. There was such power in this reality. The Word is Christ—the Christ to whom she and her Sister nuns had devoted their lives in perpetual adoration. The Word—and words—are for communication. Mother Angelica's vision was clear and powerful—communicate the Word through words and images with increasing power and commitment. The addition of television as a ministry of the monastery would now become of paramount importance, building on her written words.

It was in defense of the Word that Mother forged ahead with her plans for television, and it was the Word that inspired her to name her ministry the Eternal Word Television Network (EWTN). Ironically, it was also the blasphemous film, entitled *The Word,* that propelled Mother into the age of the electronic media.

Between 1978 and 1982, Mother Angelica would see the continued development of the Sisters' religious life at Our

Lady of the Angels Monastery, she would see her books printed and distributed in the millions, she would watch in amazement as EWTN took to the air waves—and she would be crushed by the staggering financial obligations required to build the television ministry. Perhaps most shocking of all would be criticism and rejection of EWTN from the most unexpected of sources—fellow Catholic communicators. Had she known that her simple dream to uplift Christ through the medium of television would grow into a monstrous and sometimes heartbreaking challenge, one wonders if she might not have changed her mind. But then, Mother Angelica has never been one to buckle under in the face of overwhelming odds.

"I thought I had my hands full with building a monastery and later a printing operation," Mother says. "When TV came along, I really found out what tough times are all about—but God kept stretching our faith, step by step, until we began to see Him in every struggle and watch His providence perform wonders."

As the walls of what had been meant to be a garage began to rise out of the concrete foundation, the Eternal Word Television Network studio began taking shape. Although small by industry standards, the endeavor was already producing staggering bills. The structure, lights, cameras and video equipment were ordered on pure faith.

"Our motto was becoming 'just in time,' " Sister Raphael says. "Jesus never gives us more than we need—He demands faith week by week. As we have discussed in our morning lessons together, when God gives us an opportunity to do something for Him, and we have agreed that it is His apparent will, we must act in faith or the opportunity is lost. Even though some on the outside thought that getting into television was just an ego trip for Mother, we recognized the unmistakable urging of the Holy Spirit within our community. It is better to appear foolish before men than to answer to God for being afraid to step out and trust Him. And God has always provided—just in time."

Mother Angelica agrees. "I began to watch God evolve the situation and as a door opened, I stepped through, even though reason rebelled at the risk and the debt that had to be assumed. I was shaking inside and scared to death the first time I ordered television equipment. As the cost loomed before me and I saw the impossibility of being able to pay by any human standards, I was overwhelmed by the responsibility involved. I can't tell you how many times I had my hand on the telephone to call and cancel the order, but each time something would happen to call me away from it. Some big company would be willing to give credit with no more collateral than my signature, or there would be an opportunity to borrow at low interest. You know," Mother continues, "one of my many definitions of faith is 'one foot in the air, one on the ground, and a queasy feeling in your stomach.' I take a lot of Maalox. Someone once challenged me saying that if I were a person of such great faith I wouldn't need Maalox. I told her that my stomach doesn't know I have faith!"

Installments of equipment began to arrive at Our Lady of the Angels Monastery with a price tag of more than $100,000. Payment appeared totally out of reach, but then things began to happen. The Italian lighting company that provided the studio lighting reduced their price from $48,000 to $14,000. The camera, valued at $24,000, was paid for by offerings taken on one of Mother's speaking tours. She found the generosity encouraging—and overwhelming.

"I want everything done yesterday!" Mother Angelica exclaimed to a rapt audience. "There's no Italian who is born patient."

"Mother Angelica has a rare kind of charisma," explains one of the Sisters. "She is recognized as holy but also very human. People gather hope for their own souls as they listen to her humorous description of everyday happenings here in the monastery.''

One person in attendance at a Mother Angelica meeting turned out to be a staff member from the PTL Network, a highly successful Protestant Christian television ministry run by Jim Bakker. Mother soon found herself with an invitation to be on a PTL live satellite program. In January of 1979 Mother Angelica stepped in front of the PTL cameras, the first Catholic nun to do so. Bakker, an Assembly of God minister, was visibly cautious in his interview at first. But within minutes, Mother warmed up the studio audience and the millions of television viewers with her charm, her wit and humor. She was invited back to the studio many times and was later listed as among the top ten most popular guests to have appeared on PTL.

"I'll never forget interviewing Mother Angelica," says author and television cohost Doug Wead. "I was substituting for Jim when Mother Angelica came on and I was absolutely amazed at Mother's personal charm, energy and dynamism. I think one of the reasons she proved so successful on the PTL Network is that her faith is so pure, simple and rock-solid— she knows exactly what she believes and why she believes it. She was a knockout!''

By this time, Mother had produced more than ninety half-hour programs which were sent throughout the country to cable stations, hospitals and prisons, where they have become permanent library material. By April of 1979, it became apparent that more space—and equipment—would be necessary to produce quality programs. A crew of five talented young technicians, some of them longtime friends of Mother and the Sisters, came together to form a tight, professional production team. Among them were Virginia (Ginny) Dominick and Matt Scalici. Both have touching stories of Mother's personal involvement in their lives and both have worked tirelessly to put their mark of excellence on EWTN.

"When I look back over these past several years, I'm amazed at what has happened," says Matt Scalici, senior vice president of engineering and satellite operations. "Mother would tell me to do something—buy some equipment or modify the telephone system—and I would say, okay Mother, it's going to take us six to nine months. But Mother would say, 'Impossible! We need it now!' I honestly didn't see any way I could do some of the things that have been done, not just technically, but financially. Sometimes it has been highly frustrating and sometimes Mother will chew me out good when something's not just exactly right, but I'm ready for that because she's so loving and so committed to all of us. She's an amazing woman and it seems like miracles just keep happening."

Ginny Dominick's family has known Mother Angelica and the Sisters for many years. Ginny, an executive vice president, is an accomplished producer and media professional who experienced a spiritual renewal after years of disillusionment. Mother Angelica held the keys of faith for her.

"I reached a point of tragedy and sorrow in my life as my sister was dying of an inoperable brain tumor," Ginny recalls. "There were many well-meaning charismatic Christians who were praying for and claiming healing for my sister—including me. They all said she'll be just fine. God will heal her. Then along came Mother Angelica. She understands pain, she understands sorrow and she knows how suffering often works in our lives. She gave me no assurance that Sara would live, and that was tough for me to handle. I was perplexed that Mother had no easy answers, but her words of wisdom ultimately helped me live with Sara's death in 1978. She didn't give me false hope—she gave me reality based on her faith and years of spiritual insight. When she asked me to come to work for her, at first I declined, but after an inner struggle I decided to go to work for EWTN. It was the Lord that led me back to Mother Angelica."

Ginny, a frequent traveling companion and friend of Mother Angelica, sees another side of the television nun. "So many people see the miracles that have happened in Mother's ministry. They see the network, they know how God has miraculously provided, and they'll see Mother traveling and speaking. But I can tell you from experience, I know the pain and agony that Mother endures. Many people don't know that she has a serious heart condition, which she rarely talks about, along with her leg and back problems, all of which produce constant and sometimes severe pain. I have seen her exhausted, hurting and nearly overwhelmed by her dizzying schedule, yet she continues and she will make herself available to those who recognize her. People don't know the price she's paid."

And how does Mother Angelica deal with the rise from anonymity in the cloister to fame through television? "It's been extremely interesting to watch," answers Ginny. "At first, people would run up to her, recognizing her in airports, and she would be completely surprised and a little overwhelmed. She has since become accustomed to this, but has still never thought of herself as any kind of celebrity. Mother has always said that it's not failure in the television industry that scares her the most—it's success. She knows what it can do to people."

On September 18, 1980, Mother Angelica ordered a satellite dish and applied for a Federal Communications Commission license to broadcast. A satellite network was just what she needed to make her programing available for families and various Catholic organizations, as well as Christians at large, who could not afford other forms of programing.

"Her real desire is to feed the people of God—this has been her constant incentive," Sister Raphael says. "She has found people to be hungering for His Word and His truth. She desires to tell the world about Jesus who is present in the Holy Eucharist. Seeing young people come here with no concept of the indwelling of the Trinity in their souls, seeing them risk destroying this temple of the Holy Spirit with drugs and alcohol, make her realize that the heart of Jesus is wounded and that she has a moral obligation to spread the truth in every way possible."

Mother knew she had to push ahead with a satellite system. She wanted the most advanced technology available to glorify God. She was committed to the long haul and to the cost—which would be substantial. "I didn't know the first thing about the FCC," Mother says. "But I knew I needed an attorney so I simply looked up an attorney with an Italian-sounding name in Washington, D.C., and called. The application procedure is extremely complicated—there are all kinds of laws you have to deal with—but we managed, with God's help."

Indeed, it seemed that there would be no stopping Mother Angelica and EWTN. Soon the news was out on the streets that a cloistered nun was building a television network of stellar proportions.

Not all received the news with rejoicing. Whispers of criticism were heard among high-ranking Catholic officials who had begun to establish their own electronic-media systems. The Catholic Telecommunications Network of America (CTNA) is a for-profit subsidiary of the U.S. Catholic Conference. Although millions of dollars had been budgeted and scores of experts were involved, it seemed to many—both within and outside of CTNA—that things were progressing painfully slow. Designed to disseminate television and radio programs to affiliated Catholic dioceses, CTNA also hoped to provide teleconferencing and electronic mail, improving the church's entire internal communications system. Some in the CTNA system, and other Roman Catholic media endeavors, were chagrined by Mother Angelica's motto for EWTN: "The Catholic Television Network."

"Why doesn't she go back to the cloister where she belongs," one official was heard to say. "She'll never make it in the world of television—EWTN will go under in less than a year.''

Mother and the Sisters were shattered. They couldn't believe that there were some in their own church who did not accept her mission and others who seemed bent on destroying it.

"I don't think anybody really knows how devastated Mother was over this," Ginny Dominick says. "I think it is one of the hardest things that Mother has had to bear—more than all the physical pain. Again, it was a major rejection in her life and a devastating blow."

And why the resistance from the official Catholic media world? "I think there were a number of points of concern," reports one priest, an official with CTNA. "Mother Angelica proceeded without official authorization and with her own funds. You can't do these things in a vacuum—it affects all the rest of us who are attempting to utilize the media in an appropriate fashion. And, frankly, we wondered how she could handle the huge costs involved, since she claims she has no consistent flow of money from large donors. Where does it come from? Then there was the question of duplication—why should we be on two satellites, paying twice as much? Personally, I appreciate Mother Angelica but let's face it, she's a very simple nun with no sophistication when it comes to television programing. There's no way her stuff is going to play in sophisticated media centers like New York. Maybe in the Midwest. But not New York. But I must say this—I believe there are needs she is filling, among some viewers, that CTNA cannot fill."

Sources close to Mother Angelica have other ideas about reasons her network has been discounted. "It's simple," one staff member says. "Some people are jealous! They can't stand the thought of trying to get their own programing off the ground while Mother Angelica moves out ahead with the first Catholic television network on satellite."

"Look," Mother Angelica observes, "I don't know why God chose me. I'm a nobody. God just uses me to move ahead in stubborn, obstinate obedience. Someday—and maybe soon—I'm gonna wear out and God will find someone else to continue this work. Look at the scriptures! He has always used the simple to confound the mighty and the weak rather than the strong. It's like David and Goliath—we're taking on a major media world with a slingshot and a few stones, but we're making it happen.''

As word of Mother Angelica's satellite television system spread, the secular media sat up to take notice. Intrigued by this project, a reporter from *The Wall Street Journal* arrived at the monastery the very day the satellite dish arrived. He spent an entire day speaking with Mother and the Sisters and wrote a very positive article that reached many who were unaware of the progress of EWTN. The article, which appeared on Thursday, March 19, 1981, carried the following headline: "Mother Angelica Has a Job for Heaven in a Secular World." *Wall Street Journal* staff reporter Chester Goolrick reported that "We've had the singing nun and the flying nun; now comes the broadcasting nun." His article went on:

> In an era when Bible-thumping broadcasters appear daily on America's air waves with apocalyptic sermons and political exhortations, Christian television is a highly visible phenomenon. Even so, Mother Angelica stands out
>
> For one thing, she has been able to obtain the first FCC license ever granted a monastic order to operate a television station. For another, she plans to avoid using her TV pulpit for temporal pronouncements.
>
> "Our network is going to dwell on the spiritual and social aspects," she says. "I don't see Jesus involved in the political process."

Soon a call came from "Good Morning America," and another one from Newsweek Video and *The New York Post. People*

Magazine and network news broadcasts were scrambling to tell the story.

Just prior to the installation of the thirty-three–foot diameter satellite dish, a critical moment emerged and the Sisters gathered for emergency prayer. Sister Regina had an amazing vision in which she saw a black sky, a white satellite dish and a flame emerging from its center. She heard the Father say, "This is my network and it will glorify my Son."

"This was a tremendous consolation for all of us," Sister Raphael remembers. "A few weeks later the satellite dish arrived. We all crowded into our backyard, along with the crew, to watch a crane install the dish. The day was perfect with blue skies and white clouds—it was high noon. One of the boys—Matt Scalici's brother—was riding on the crane, swinging high in the air near the dish. Matt shot several pictures of him swinging from a leather belt. When the film was developed and presented to Mother, she became ecstatic. There on the photo was the black sky of the vision, the white dish in the background and a red flame emerging from its center."

Indeed, the photograph is chilling to see. It has been examined, along with the negative, by professional photographers and none can account for the radiant flame-like shaft of light that seems to rise up out of the dish into an inexplicably darkened sky. Mother calls it a miracle. It's hard to argue with her. It was another wondrous grace appropriated by Mother as she proceeded with her plans. Months would be required to assemble the components necessary for satellite transmission.

The increasing media exposure of Mother Angelica also continued to produce more criticism and pressure. One of the severest emotional setbacks for Mother and the Sisters came in the form of word that Mother would have to leave the cloister if she wished to continue her television work. A number of the Sisters report that this was among the greatest of crises faced by Mother Angelica, because her very vocation was threatened by what she believed God had told her to do.

"The greatest single crisis in the formation of EWTN came when people spoke lies about Mother and tried to destroy the network. They asked her to become a lay person if she really wanted to have a TV network, and that she would not do! That broke her heart," says Sister Emmanuel.

Sister Grace Marie agrees: "Our biggest crisis came with the lack of acceptance by those who really should have been most supportive." Sisters Catherine and Sharbel agree that lack of ecclesiastical cooperation was most difficult to bear.

It was apparent that Mother needed friends in high places and she was about to get them. On May 21, 1981, Cardinal Oddi, head of the Sacred Congregation for the Clergy in Rome, visited Our Lady of the Angels Monastery at the invitation of Bill Steltemeier, who had become president of the network's board of governors. Mother led Cardinal Oddi through the network complex and he was visibly impressed by all he saw.

"This is the only satellite network the Catholic Church has in the world!" he told her. The cardinal promised to see the pope on the following day and tell him of Mother Angelica's progress in putting together a Catholic network. He later described his visit to the monastery as the highlight of his trip to America. Cardinal Oddi assured Mother Angelica and the Sisters that he would soon have the required permissions needed to carry out the broadcasting work God had given Mother to do, protecting her status as a cloistered nun. Mother was overcome with gratitude.

Cardinal Oddi wrote a tribute in Italian in the Sisters' guest book while at the monastery:

> I am happy to bless this initiative which will undoubtedly produce abundant fruits in the field of evangelization. Since the Lord has permitted human beings to discover

some of the secrets of nature, the Church should be the first to utilize the modern methods of transmission. May the Lord reward most generously this small group of consecrated nuns who have dedicated themselves with such strong faith to the accomplishment of this work.

Silvio Cardinal Oddi
Prefect of the Sacred Congregation
for the Clergy,
May 21, 1981

Encouragement also came from other church officials such as Bernard Cardinal Law, archbishop of Boston, who would later write in a letter that Mother Angelica has fulfilled the mandate of the church in its decree on the instruments of social communication with capable and courageous leadership. He has highly recommended the support of EWTN.

While Mother has enlisted other allies in her cause, the greatest encouragement has come from the providence of God, who she now recognizes had some kind of communications plan for her life from the very beginning of her vocation. It is no accident to Mother Angelica that the patron saint of television is Saint Clare, foundress of the Poor Clares (Franciscan nuns).

"There was an incident in the life of Saint Clare that took place when she was very sick. She wanted to attend a Christmas Eve Mass but could not go. Instead, she literally saw the Mass through the walls of her room, as if by some miraculous television-like transmission," Mother Angelica says.

"And there's an even more amazing story about my name," she continues, "my name is Mother Mary Angelica and my title is 'of the Annunciation.' The Annunciation, historically, was done by Gabriel, the archangel. Gabriel is also the patron saint of television and communications along with Saint Clare! What's even more interesting is the fact that my superior, Mother Agnes, picked March 25, the feast of the Annunciation, as my feast day instead of the Holy Angels, as is normally the case. This put strong emphasis, from the beginning, on television, communications and generally announcing the faith. That is now being done through the Eternal Word Television Network.''

God's providence and His grace have comforted Mother through the firestorm of adversity and criticism. She has needed every ounce of it. She would need more for the future. Her financial challenges were only about to begin.

As mid-August of 1981 approached, work at Our Lady of the Angels Monastery had reached a fever pitch. Mother was on top of every move—she directed construction crews as they raced to complete work on the EWTN satellite uplink system, she motivated and encouraged her loyal production crew as they familiarized themselves with their new equipment and she put the Sisters through their prayer paces as the big countdown continued. There could be no turning back now.

Somehow, while the experts continued to scratch their heads in amazement, all the components of the EWTN network coalesced around a little monastery in a small suburb of Birmingham, Alabama. Legally, everything had to be perfect and in line with government regulations. Technically, systems and expertise were required to transmit a high-powered signal to a satellite transponder in order to blanket the country with EWTN programing material. Creatively, video productions would be required to fill four nightly hours of air time, seven days a week, in order to continue telecasting.

Financially, the price tag for all of this would be staggering, and Mother knew it. She felt she had no choice. Even though there were insufficient funds to purchase transponder time, Mother pushed forward relentlessly in the kind of brinkmanship for which she had become well known. Each component came together in a critical mass which, on August 15, 1981, would result in an explosion—Our Lady of the Angels Monastery, EWTN and Mother Angelica would become known from coast to coast, and far beyond. Mother Angelica would make media history.

As that day approached, the monastery telephones began ringing off their hooks. NBC's "Today Show" invited Mother Angelica to appear for an interview. ABC's "Good Morning America" rushed forward also asking for a guest appearance. *PM Magazine,* CNN and CBS scrambled to cover the breaking story of the cloistered nun who had somehow done the impossible. There was even a European TV crew present to take the story back to Europe, where Mother Angelica was beginning to receive a significant amount of press.

On the afternoon of August 15, Mother Angelica, awaiting the arrival of her many guests, walked into the new studio filled with emotion. She greeted Mike Mooney, designer of the control room, and each of her young crew with a glowing smile and tears in her eyes. She expressed her boundless appreciation for their tremendous sacrifices. They had worked through the night scheduling programs, editing video material and testing all the equipment.

"Thank you!" Mother said with a trembling voice, tears bursting forth. She hugged each crew member. They wept openly, exhausted but filled with anticipation.

Deep within the monastery, in the chapel where so many thousands of hours of prayer had ascended before the Blessed Sacrament, a procession gathered. Christ, the Eternal Word, was hidden in the Host above the altar. There was a long moment of prayerful silence as each participant realized that the Word was about to go forth to millions through space-age technology and the commitment of a handful of nuns.

A cross-bearer, flag-bearers and the nuns moved together from the monastery followed by the board of governors of the network and the crew. Bishop Joseph Vath and special guests

followed. They walked triumphantly to the door of the studio
control room where Mother turned to face the gathering with
a prayer she composed:

> Oh God, Lord of Heaven and Earth, You alone have ac-
> complished all we have done. May this first Catholic satellite
> television network be a tribute to the beauty of Your
> Church. May Your Son, the Eternal Word, be glorified
> through this work of your Hands. Bless all the programs
> that will issue forth from its facilities. Just as Your Word
> issued forth from You, Lord Father, may that same Word
> touch each heart that listens to this network. Let Thy Spirit
> work with freedom through every teacher who proclaims
> Thy truth and Thy Church. Bestow upon this network the
> power to inspire men to seek holiness of heart, zeal for the
> extension of Thy Church, courage to seek after justice and
> human rights and patience to endure persecution.

Mother snipped the ribbon outside of the control room and
walked slowly inside. There was spontaneous singing as the
big moment approached. After a silent prayer, the countdown
began: five, four, three, two, one. An uproarious cheer burst
forth from all as Mother Angelica threw the switch that sent
EWTN's first program skyward. It was exactly 6:00 P.M.

Throughout this special day there was one Sister who stayed
close by Mother Angelica's side and, during the procession
and telecast ceremony, Mother held her hand tightly. It was
Sister David, now confined to a wheelchair. Mother Angelica's aging mother had broken her hip in a fall that forced her
to spend fourteen of her twenty years in the monastery in a
wheelchair. She maintained an active role in the ministry,
sorting through mail and supporting the mini-book ministry
by handling correspondence.

On August 22, 1982, Sister David of the Infant Jesus died.
She was laid to rest in a small chapel in the monastery where
Mother Angelica still frequently goes to pray.

✳

Christ's miracle of the loaves and fishes fed thousands. Somehow, Mother Angelica multiplied $200 into $2 million in television equipment to spiritually feed millions. Mother Angelica's dream had come true.

"I can hardly believe it myself!" Mother Angelica exclaims. "Two years ago I was a cloistered nun who couldn't even adjust the color on our own TV. Now we have $2 million in video equipment! Doesn't God have a great sense of humor looking for people like us to do His work?"

Indeed, Mother Angelica's accomplishments are astounding by anyone's measurement. Even those in official Catholic communications circles were impressed with EWTN and began taking a second look, particularly after media trade journals reported that the network was the fastest-growing cable system in America.

Success, however, did not come without its staggering price. In order to pay for satellite time, underwrite video productions and manage the fast-growing network, the monastery needed hundreds of thousands of dollars per month to stay on the air. The stress and pressure became, at times, almost too much to bear but God, according to the nuns of Our Lady of the Angels Monastery, continued to provide in the most miraculous ways imaginable. Anonymous checks arrived in the mail, grants were made by Catholic foundations and somehow the bills were paid, even if occasionally overdue.

In spite of the emotional drain created by her many obligations, Mother maintained her sharp sense of humor. "I was in Las Vegas one day attending a cable-television convention and was on my way to do the 'Mike Douglas Show,' " she remembers. "I walked past 150 slot machines where there was a great big transparent bowl filled with coins. It was $265,000!

I had the worst temptation to put a buck in that machine, because that's exactly the amount I needed at the time!''

Mother also amazed interviewers with her frank, to-the-point comments on her ministry. "We want to help people live holy lives," Mother Angelica pointed out to one interviewer. "You know, sometimes life stinks—you need hope to get through it and we're here to give people hope."

Frequently, casual observers have expressed incredulity that a small band of nuns could have erected a major television network. To Mother Angelica, it is no great mystery.

"Why shouldn't we do great things for God? All we have to do is recognize that it's really God in us, working through us. Remember," Mother Angelica reminds, "the Lord gave the Israelites the best artists, craftsmen and materials to build a temple. The same God is guiding and instructing us to day."

Just about the time those working with Mother began to relax from their exhaustion, she saw a new frontier that had to be conquered. She looked ahead and realized that a small, garage-sized studio would simply not be enough room for productions she knew would have to be done. She pushed ahead with ambitious plans to build a new, larger studio, complete with office space and state-of-the-art equipment.

"Of course, I knew we didn't have the money," Mother Angelica says. "But we never do. It comes when you need it. I walked outside where I knew the studio would be built and marched around that acreage like Joshua, claiming it for the Lord. I asked the maintenance man to mark trees where the studio would be. He tied white rags around each tree. People would walk up to me and ask, 'Mother, what are all of those rags doing on the trees?' I told them I was just reminding God about the studio that would someday be there!"

There was no question about the fact that big money would be needed to build a studio. But once again, the loyal

Sisters went to their knees in prayer, determined that Mother would have her studio. The very name of the network gave them hope, strength and faith. They looked to Jesus. The Eternal Word.

CHAPTER NINE

————— ✳ —————

Gabriel

Mass in the chapel of Our Lady of the Angels Monastery on April 14, 1985, was anything but routine. EWTN supporters had gathered from across the nation to join in celebrating the grand opening of Mother Angelica's new studio. It looked like rain, a potential disaster for the outdoor procession and ribbon-cutting ceremony. But, of course, the Sisters' prayers prevailed and the threatening clouds parted directly above the facility. Long shafts of light filtered down upon the happy event.

Cars with out-of-state license plates wheeled into the grounds under the watchful eyes of Irondale police who packed crackling walkie-talkies. They appeared just a little out of place in the monastery parking lot. A carload of Dominican nuns, an assortment of New York executives, a scattering of priests and the ubiquitous brown Franciscan habits flowed together into a joyful celebration which some had doubted would actually come to pass.

After pumping hands and dispensing a host of hugs, Mother moved with purpose through the crowd of well-wishers and whispered her oft-heard injunction, "Let's get on with it!"

Singing Sisters marched behind Mother Angelica who was armed with the ribbon-cutting scissors. A priest began the dedication proceedings, consecrating the new building for service unto God. With a prayer and a snip, thunderous ap-

141

plause was directed skyward and the multitude marched into the new fifty by seventy–foot studio.

The new building includes a conference room, workshop and marketing offices which, while smartly finished, are nonetheless plain and unpretentious. Grants from the Koch Foundation, the Catholic Extension Society, the Knights of Columbus, Jack and Ruth Ledger and Pittsburgh businessman Frank Schnieder helped to underwrite the ambitious project. Many donors were on hand to rejoice with the Sisters and crew as yet one more giant fell before Mother's whirling sling. A state-of-the-art studio had replaced Mother's ragwrapped pine trees.

With the consecration of the new EWTN studio, a new era had dawned for Mother Angelica's work. She now had all the hardware and space to produce quality programs for the network. The software—the creative productions on video tape— would now become a primary focus of her labors, for without programing, the network would not survive. It would be like an exotic stereo system with no albums on the shelf. Television is even more demanding because while record albums are made to be heard repeatedly, video programing must be constantly fresh. This creates pressure to produce an endless supply of product to educate viewers and to perpetuate the ministry.

"This isn't something we can't handle," Mother asserts vigorously. "I look at it as a tremendous opportunity for collaboration—for working together with other ministries to further God's kingdom. They will help provide the programing."

Standing outside of the studio on the day of its dedication, Mother Angelica looked tiny in comparison to the warehouse-sized structure. Hands on hips, she stood back and looked up at the building. The preceding four years, while immensely exciting for the Sisters and the EWTN crew, had nevertheless taken a tremendous toll on Mother. She was beginning to show the strain. At the end of the day, she limped back to the cloister exhausted, her back pain beginning to flare up.

*

Much had happened between that moment in 1981, when Mother threw the switch bouncing her EWTN signal off of a satellite, and the dedication of the new studio facility only three and one-half years later. The sheer volume of work generated at the monastery was almost unbelievable—the printing operation continued, faster than ever, under the direction of a small group of Sisters who had joined forces with some of Mother's EWTN crew, linking the print and electronic-media ministries. On top of this, EWTN produced, coproduced and aired hundreds of programs ranging from older family oriented reruns to commentaries by Catholic theologians. The buzz of activity never subsides. There is always something being produced, edited or aired and, somehow, Mother Angelica stays on top of it all.

By far the most popular program produced by EWTN is "Mother Angelica Live." On this call-in program, Mother Angelica features special guests who have included entertainer Pat Boone, Cardinal Bernard Law, Father Bruce Ritter, Cardinal Oddi and many others. She obviously hit a responsive chord with the public. By spring of 1983 EWTN was reaching more than 1 million homes. While many associated with the network were understandably elated, Mother took it in stride.

"I look upon that million as a million among millions," she says. "It's the first step up the ladder. Not a ladder of success, but the ladder to the people. We're trying to reach people. We want to reach every nook and cranny in the country. We want to reach hospitals and prisons—all the places where there are people in spiritual need. We are not interested in just adding subscribers. We want those people we have now, and all those millions that we hope to add in the future, to be able to say that we have the best four hours on television. What we really want to do is reach that *one* in a million—that *one* person. We are interested in the individual. One woman wrote to me the other day and said she watches our network every night—she says she feels like she has died and gone to heaven. You can't feel much more at home than that!"

Franciscan singer-songwriter John Michael Talbot has appeared on EWTN numerous times. A successful media professional in his own right, Talbot marvels at Mother Angelica's successes.

"I can remember when I first heard of Mother Angelica," Talbot says. "She was believing God to pay the bills and she was stepping out in faith for major things like video equipment, air time and production expenses. I was a little dubious at first— we've all heard of these faith ministries who claim God is telling them to proceed with major programs of one kind or another, and then the bills go unpaid. It didn't take me long to see, however, that God was, in a very real way, honoring Mother Angelica's faith. It has been truly amazing to see how things have come together. The woman gets results."

Indeed, Mother Angelica's strong faith has produced remarkable results, but she is quick to point out that she is only human and, from time to time, reaches her limits.

"The Lord lets me go through anxieties and frustrations— this work can be incredibly hair-raising at times. I have to admit, my list for confession has grown considerably since I met television! There are times when I have questioned myself and God. There have been times when I wanted to throw the crew out the window along with my Sisters and the equipment! At times I have been just frustrated to death, but I feel this is part of faith. I think it's the only way God can do great things," Mother says.

While she and the EWTN crew continue to strive for excellence, Mother Angelica sometimes bridles against some of the restrictions of media professionalism. "Everything today evolves around feasibility studies," she says with a hint of exasperation. "Just suppose Jesus had decided to do a feasibility study on whether or not He should have chosen those twelve apostles."

Mother Angelica continues to charge ahead with a heart full of dreams, little money in her pocket and loads of faith, the likes of which is rarely seen. Many in the media around the country are sitting up to take notice. Since going on the air in 1981, Mother Angelica and EWTN have been widely reported on in *The Los Angeles Times, The New York Times, People Magazine, Variety, The Washington Post, USA Today, National Geographic, US News and World Report,* and a seemingly endless list of other publications. As EWTN continues to grow in its impact, she finds herself making appearances on such television programs as "The Mike Douglas Show," "Hour Magazine," ABC's "World News Tonight," and return appearances on the major Christian television networks. She even appeared on "Dick Clark's TV Bloopers" in November of 1984, her sense of humor shining bright as ever.

Mother Angelica received an honorary doctorate of sacred theology from the University of Steubenville in 1983 and an honorary doctor of letters degree from the University of St. Thomas, Houston, in 1984. Mother's awards are numerous and include Morality in Media's Woman of the Year in 1982, the John Paul II Religious Freedom Award given by the Catholic League for Religious and Civil Rights in 1983, and the 1985 Citizen of the Year Award from the Alabama Cable Television Associates. The list goes on.

This recognition, however, seems to mean little to Mother Angelica or the Sisters—one almost never hears the commendations mentioned. There is one citation, however, that has meant as much as all the others combined: the Gabriel Award. This award, given in the form of an Oscar-like statuette, is presented annually to individuals as well as radio and television stations that provide programs "of excellence in support of positive human values."

The prestigious awards are presented by the National Association of Catholic Broadcasters and Allied Communicators during the annual general assembly of Unda-USA. Mother Angelica received the 1984 Gabriel Personal Achievement Award in December. Those who have received the award include Helen Hayes, Bill Moyers, Walter Cronkite, Charles Osgood and other media achievers.

"Mother Angelica's contribution has been to build a national Catholic network. She began with faith, dedication and the commitment of a small number of her own Sisters. That's an outstanding contribution to the industry and the people who watch television by anybody's definition," said Unda-USA President Father John Geaney, as he presented the award to Mother Angelica during the Gabriel ceremonies in Boston. There was loud, standing applause.

Mother and other EWTN executives in attendance were overwhelmed and honored. It was a sign of acceptance from her peers in the Catholic communications community. "Finally," one of her associates pointed out that evening, "Mother is being recognized for her achievements by those most important to her."

Dr. Maury Sheridan, the current president of Unda-USA, was in attendance at the award banquet that night. "That evening made it known that Mother Angelica had truly earned her place—the award was well deserved," Sheridan says. "I must say that a Gabriel Award truly takes on more stature because of people like Mother Angelica. Not long after that general session I went down to visit her at the monastery—I felt that I got to know her and EWTN better. What most impresses me is the tremendous theology of risk she embraces. She is truly a woman of faith."

During his trip to the monastery, the Unda president, who also serves as director for the office of communications in the

Seattle archdiocese, had positive discussions with Mother Angelica and her executives which covered a range of topics including previous conflicts.

"We had an excellent discussion about perceptions within
the Catholic communications community," Sheridan reports.
"I have found that people genuinely want Mother Angelica
to participate together with them as a peer—not marginally
involved, but in full collaboration and participation. The potential is exciting."

"There is no reason for competition," Mother agrees. "We
can all work together and bring the riches of the faith to the
various peoples and cultures in our country and in our world."

Mother adds that some of her critics are more concerned
with her theology than her threat in the electronic media.
"Some of these people think I'm an archconservative—they
think I'm a kind of Archbishop Lefebvre who wants to be a
slave to past tradition. That simply isn't true. I am orthodox
in my beliefs and have a deep respect for the church and our
Holy Father. Is being orthodox all that much of a crime these
days?" she asks. "Besides, what's so conservative about a
group of cloistered nuns erecting the first Catholic satellite
operation in the world?"

Mother Angelica continues, pointing out the real objectives
of EWTN: "Our goal is to serve the Holy Father and the magisterium of the church. By doing so we know we are doing God's
will. Our network is built on faith and sustained by prayer."

With costs now reaching more than $360,000 per month,
Mother Angelica's prayers are growing increasingly fervent.
Today, the network claims close to 300 cable systems reaching
9 million homes. The costs, though staggering, have been
managed—just barely—by EWTN.

In a New York press conference, in September of 1985,
Mother Angelica expressed her opinion as to why the Catholic
Church has not done more in its media endeavors. "The
Church is terrifically remiss in production," she said. "As

a church, we ought to have the most fantastic programs ever produced. But we have lost, in the church, the theology of risk," she stated emphatically. "We say, it will cost. We are so cost-minded that we don't even try."

Obviously, the exhausting demands of running a major television network have not blunted Mother's fighting spirit. She continues to move ahead vigorously, claiming new cable systems and new allies to her cause with each passing week. There seems no end in sight.

Mother Angelica seemed amazingly calm as she ushered me into the "Blue Room" in the monastery—a small living room-dining room where guests are sometimes entertained. Phones were ringing, Sisters were quickly moving through the halls and guests were arriving for the dedication of the new studio. It was April 13, 1985. Mother Angelica and I were continuing our series of interviews and, on this occasion, Mother seemed as calm as the eye of a hurricane.

She leaned forward attentively, hands clasped, legs crossed at the ankle, her leather and metal leg brace looking as though it had become a part of her. A large crucifix dangled below her smiling face—a shock of thick, gray hair disappears up into her veil. She looks every inch the Italian grandmother—complete with glasses and a hovering, matriarchal presence. One is struck by her complexion—clear and smooth. In her sixties, she has barely a wrinkle.

"Okay. What do we talk about now?" Mother asked pleasantly. She had been most cooperative, spending hours with me and turning over numerous documents, photographs and memorabilia. We had, I felt, just about covered everything. Now I had a few questions on a range of subjects.

"You inspire so many people through your writing and through your television programs. What inspires you?" I asked.

"Jesus." Mother looked at me with a radiant smile, hesitating for some moments. "Jesus inspires me. I am most inspired by what He does in other people's souls—how He shapes them and molds them into the image of Himself. Of course, that must be the goal of all of us. I am amazed at what He has done in my own life, in spite of my many failings. I'm sure He wants me—all of us—to be living saints, not in imitation of historical saints who have been canonized in the church, but ourselves. We are supposed to be ourselves—to be who Jesus really made us to be. I am inspired by this business of how God goes about making us into saints, if we will just let Him."

"How do you feel about the major Protestant television networks that have become so successful—can you relate to them ecumenically?"

"You know, when I go to the convention of the National Religious Broadcasters, I often feel we don't really belong. We stick out like a sore thumb because of our goals, theology and spirituality. Interestingly, sometimes Protestants will call or write and tell us that they think we have more depth and spirituality in our teaching. Trinity Broadcasting Network, the Christian Broadcasting Network and the PTL Network—I think they are all just a little afraid that I'll take away their Catholic contributors. But the Spirit leads them in a different way and we must be free to follow the Spirit in our own way. My mission is really pretty simple: broadcast Catholic doctrine, teaching, theology and practice. This is where we part ways with some of the Protestant networks. I know they have removed some of my programs from the air, and we have removed some of theirs from our own broadcast lineup. We have to be honest and recognize there are differences which exist among us, but there are also many similarities. Jesus must be at the center of all of our ministries.

"There is something that really bothers me and that is the new anti-Catholicism springing up around the country,"

Mother continues, her eyes squinting as she recalls an incident that damaged EWTN during a fund-raising telethon. "You know, we had telephone numbers on the screen so that people could call in and request prayer or donate to the ministry. In an orchestrated attempt to sabotage our telethon, a number of people jammed our phone lines with calls that kept others from reaching us. I was tremendously angry, but I prayed for their souls. I pray for Jack Chick who publishes all of those horrid anti-Catholic comic books. I pray for Jimmy Swaggart who has come against the Catholic Church publicly and I pray for others who are actively attacking Catholicism. I pray for those people daily. In some ways, there are benefits. It forces Catholics to know their faith—to become more familiar with the teaching of the church. No one has the right to put down another denomination to promote their own kind of Christianity. I can remember the late Archbishop Fulton Sheen, one of the great television personalities of our time, saying that every time you throw dirt at someone else, you lose your own ground. There must be a balance between righteous indignation and compassionate prayer."

"What about life issues facing the Church?" I asked, "How do you feel about the nuclear-war issue, abortion, capital punishment, poverty?"

"Our job must be to proclaim what the church teaches," Mother states flatly. "I will not air programs that are blatantly opposed to the Holy Father. But I won't hesitate to deal with real issues such as child abuse, questions on liberation theology, medical ethics—we've touched on all of these in our programs. When it comes to controversial issues like women's ordination, however, the Holy Father has spoken. You know there are two sexes—this seems to come as a surprise to some people! Worrying about sexist language is a blatantly stupid concept. Why waste time on it? I know women have had difficulties, that's true. I've had my own difficulties. Yes, there are real injustices in the church and they have hurt me at times. But I don't blame this on the church—I blame this on certain people within the church. I really believe that obedience is today's crisis. People are saying, 'I will not serve!' "

"Why do you feel, Mother Angelica, that you are sometimes condemned as an archconservative?" I asked.

Mother rocked back in her chair, throwing her arms up in the air in mock exasperation. "It's so stupid! There are those who see me wearing this brown Franciscan habit and they think because I still wear the habit in an age when so many religious women are shedding them, that I'm some kind of hopeless conservative. Some have read my books and see them as being pre-Vatican II in flavor. People see me as being true to the teaching of the magisterium. This marks us as conservatives in the eyes of some. I talk about Jesus a lot. He constantly enters my conversation. To many, this means I'm a hopeless, conservative charismatic."

"Is television really what you want to do as opposed to your life in the cloister?" I asked, hoping to see how Mother balances her active life in the media against a cloistered life of prayer and contemplation.

"I am doing television out of obedience. Honestly, it's not what I truly desire to do—it's more like a cross I have to bear," she answers. "Sometimes I can't believe that I'm actually doing it—it doesn't seem like the real me. The real me wants to study, read, pray, contemplate—to live out the call of the cloister. And I must say that we have been amazingly true to our call to the monastic life. Sure, you see a lot of people running around in cars, packing cameras, bringing in guests for the programs. You see the crew running around producing programs—you hear about people flying in and out all the time but, amazingly, we have maintained a still, quiet place behind these walls. You can ask any of the Sisters—they will all tell you. We pray five hours a day and we live out a simple Franciscan life-style. That can never be threatened. So far it has not been a problem.

"You know," Mother continues, "we can have no real fruitful activity without a lot of prayer. This network, EWTN, is built on a foundation of prayer. Without prayer, all of this would turn to nothing. I really believe that activity and spirituality cannot be separated. They must be one, particularly in this context."

As I stood to leave, Mother struggled from her chair, the metal of her leg brace banging against a lamp stand. One becomes unaware of her obvious physical frailties after having engaged in enthusiastic conversation for a few minutes. The woman's zeal, determination and energy are almost overpowering. Her force of personality readily distracts one from her health liabilities. Mother took me by the hand and walked me slowly to the door, showing me out.

"Do you think you're getting what you want, honey? I hope we're covering everything," she frets.

"We're doing just fine, Mother."

*

Mother Angelica's great success in the competitive world of electronic media has been made successful, at least in part, because of the extraordinary people who have come to her support. One needs only to look into the eyes of Jean Morris or Bill Steltemeier to find that the keys of EWTN's success come from a rigorous enthusiasm rarely found in the highest of worldly corporate structures.

"It's amazing how we got together," Steltemeier, an attorney, says. "I was attending a legal convention in Chicago on March 9, 1978. I found my way to a little, suburban church where Mother was speaking. As I sat in the back of the church, I was totally fascinated by what Mother Angelica was saying so I decided to move up to the front to see if this woman was for real. I moved down to the third pew, directly in front of her. She looked me directly in the eye, as she was speaking—

I have never had such a mystical feeling in my entire life. Curious, I went to the reception that followed, but was determined not to get involved in conversation with this nun. I kept at a distance, but said nothing. Occasionally, she would look in my direction and smile but she said nothing. Two months later, I decided to go to Birmingham and give my conscience some peace and quiet for the first time in several months—I knew I was supposed to speak with her. One of the Sisters introduced me to Mother Angelica. She just smiled nicely and said 'I wondered when you would come.' We have been working together ever since.''

What does he see as Mother Angelica's greatest strength? ''She has the tremendous ability to live in the present moment,'' he replies. ''She is constantly aware of the indwelling of the Holy Spirit in her soul and seeks only the will of God. Absolutely nothing else matters. Over the past seven years, her teachings, love and personal example have totally changed my commitment to the Lord. I have grown spiritually beyond any goals I could have ever set for myself.''

Bill Steltemeier occupies a place of importance on the EWTN board and works tirelessly to make the ministry an ongoing success. ''Whenever I am about to do some important work for the network,'' he laughs, ''Mother sends me into 'the battle' with this advice: 'pray and keep your eyes on the Lord.' ''

Some have questioned the ability of EWTN to survive without the driving, central presence of Mother Angelica. It has been predicted that without her, the work will disintegrate. Steltemeier disagrees forcefully. ''Mother Angelica and the Sisters are cornerstones. It will be very easy for the Lord to build on this cornerstone in the future. This has always been the age-old question that was asked when any new work or religious order had begun within the church. If the Sisters and this community remain faithful to their vows, and if the rest of us involved on the outside continue to be generous with our gifts and talents, we can all look forward to a tremendous future.''

Dick Stephens, EWTN vice president, agrees. "If Mother Angelica has taught us anything, it is to trust totally in God's providence. After Mother Angelica, the Lord will deliver!''

Mother's chief source of moral support, of course, comes from her Sisters. They are, she says, a constant source of joy to her. Many of them are immensely talented and work diligently on behalf of the network or the ongoing printing ministry. As was clearly evident in the CBS "Sixty Minutes" feature on Mother Angelica, which aired in the fall of 1985, the Sisters are blessed with enthusiasm beyond limits and a bountiful sense of humor. Morley Safer was captivated by their goodness, commitment and spiritual drive. When asked what they think lies in store for Mother Angelica, many share an identical answer that one senses is more serious than facetious: "Sainthood!" they say.

*

Our Lady of the Angels Monastery is the site of something special. An ancient order of the Catholic Church coexists with a high-tech communications environment. Somehow, this improbable collision of antiquity and technology, which happens in a little-known Birmingham suburb, works. None of it was likely to happen—but it did. Mother Angelica and her devoted Sisters stroll quietly and prayerfully on their grounds in the shadow of a towering satellite dish, and they accept the paradox without question. It's simple. After all, it's God's will, they will tell you.

The world's leading experts are now looking at the next generation of electronic-media advancements. Computer technology and satellite systems are merging to create opportunities previously beyond our reach. Undoubtedly, the next major breakthrough will be met with this enthusiastic little nun clapping her hands gleefully saying, ''Lord—I gotta have one of those!'' When that happens, watch out. A radical plan will be hatched in the inner sanctum of Mother's monastery. And it will probably come to pass.

Mother Angelica, however, seems unimpressed by her accomplishments. ''I'm just God's donkey pulling this load for a while,'' she often repeats. ''When God shows us what to do next, well, we will just move on to whatever that is. Imagine! God using me!'' she exclaims, laughing, as together we look at two photographs. In one shot Mother is handing a replica of her satellite dish to Pope John Paul II in the Vatican. In the other, she is chatting with Ronald Reagan. Mother looks up and smiles. ''Just imagine that!''